My Mom's Letters
From Heaven

GERRY KLASSEN

Copyright © 2013 by Gerry Klassen

My Mom's Letters From Heaven

by Gerry Klassen

Printed in the United States of America

ISBN 9781628711462

Unless otherwise indicated, Bible quotations are taken from The Holy Bible, New International Version. Copyright 1973, 1978, 1984 by International Bible Society.

www.xulonpress.com

DEDICATION

To my wife Anne and my sister Verna without whose convincing, pressing, shoving, pushing, promoting, jabbing, provoking, urging, spurring, compelling, encouraging, coercing and goading, this book would never have been finished.

After all, like my wife said that if God could use a donkey to speak, He certainly could use you to write a book.

WORDS OF ENCOURAGEMENT

*ecently I was with a group and we read a few of Gerry's emails from his mother in Heaven. We got to thinking about those coming from our mothers. These emails made our blessed hope so real! Just thinking about them seeing the face of Jesus brought tears to our eyes, tears of hope and joy. *Rachael*

Stood and cried at a cosmetic counter this afternoon just talking with the clerk about Gerry's emails from Mom. She came out from behind the counter to give me a hug and thanked me for sharing the thoughts and what a blessing they were to her and, she imagines, to so many others, too. *Rachael*

A great read for adults and children alike to get us excited for what is to come. *Boyd*

Gerry creatively describes what Heaven just may be like-but we won't know till we get there! I love how he helps me imagine God's eternal world in everyday terms that I can relate to within my earthly dimensions. *Elisa*

I find his God given writing a gift and a joy. I have received much comfort in his words. *Carol*

I always love it when other brothers and sisters in Christ put a "face" on our Savior that I can relate to. *Donna*

So beautiful! It gives peace, love and joy to anyone who reads or hears it. Praise God for all His blessings. *Ellen*

Words of inspiration to everyone who has any doubts about after life. *Denise*

TABLE OF CONTENTS

FROM THE AUTHOR

―――⊱⊰―――

I wonder what Heaven is like. Have you ever asked yourself that question? Well, join us on a parable journey to visit with my mom who just arrived there and who writes me everyday and reports back what she does all day long. Jesus said, "I go and prepare a place for you and where I am you may be also." When the King of Kings, the God who created everything, when the Master Builder who owns the earth and the universe and everything in it, builds HIMSELF a place to live and invites you to join Him and live with Him, what do you think THAT place looks like? Go with mom and Barsuvius, her personal angel, as she leaves her old, worn body and travels on his white stallion up to the gates of Paradise, where she throws herself into the arms of her waiting family. Hear the angel Gabriel, who is carrying the Book of Life and says to her, "Jesus is waiting to see you."

Meet King David who teaches little boys how to build and shoot slingshots and tells great stories. Visit with Job who's been waiting over two thousand years for his first patient in his psychiatric office. Join Mom as she talks to angels at a local pool hall and they tell her what angels are all about and describe the reaction that the young virgin, Mary, had when Gabriel told her that she would bear a Son and He is the Son of God. Get on board a half-sized open top train of happy squealing children and find out where they got the watermelon they are sharing. Talk to Lazarus, the man whose first Paradise visit was cut short, who was raised from the dead and listen to his explanation of why that may not be the entire story. Join the guys on their Harley motorcycle trip to the top of the mountain and listen to their four-part harmony as they sing another new soul into Paradise. Listen to the lady at the well as she sings her story of living water, from a well that never runs dry.

Meet my mother's family, who were eagerly waiting at Heaven's Gate, along with the million and a half member choir who sing in new arrivals 24/7 when they come Home. Talk to Simon Peter who is a ski instructor and who, two thousand years ago, walked on water. Watch the lions and tigers and bears play with the children. See mom's new body, a new being, and hear how she is perfectly loved by the inventor of love.

Personally meet Jesus, who calls Himself the Great I Am, the First and the Last, the Beginning and the End. Watch as mom walks with Him hand in hand in the early morning through His beautiful garden and asks Him for the answers to the why questions most pressing on her heart like, "WHY ME, LORD? What have I ever done to deserve any of this?" Hear mom's encouragement to her prodigal son that he receive the Savior she serves and not miss the most fun place that any mind could ever imagine. Come take this journey with me, it sometimes brings laughter, it sometimes brings tears, and sometimes it brings surprises...

Come with me on this journey; maybe, just maybe, you will never be the same.

INTRODUCTION

---

*I*t was very early, in fact, it was before dawn, and I was sleeping soundly when I heard her and felt her standing beside the bed. "Gerry," my wife said, "Gerry." I woke but didn't move. Why was she standing there and why was she waking me so early? Very little good news ever comes to a parent in the middle of the night. All she whispered was that my sister Margaret had called. Nothing more needed to be said. That was the phone call that I had wished for, prayed for but still never wanted to hear. I didn't move. I did not really want to hear the rest of that sentence. I thought; just don't say the rest of the words, not just yet, please. I let out a half groan, half sigh, just enough to let her know that I heard her, and to indicate to her that to say anymore was unnecessary. I got up out of bed and we came together and we wrapped our arms around each other and just sobbed. My beloved mother had died!

The day was full of phone calls about arrangements and discussion about the last day's events. I continued my business that day, putting on a brave face for my clients. Very early the next morning, it was probably 4:30 or so, I was awakened and it was like someone was dictating a letter in my head. I got up, grabbed a paper and pen, and as quickly as I could, started writing. What am I doing, why am I writing a letter that's coming from my mother who has just passed away? Why am I doing this? It was almost like a compulsion! I wrote down things that were being given to me as fast as I could because some of the words were fading. I grabbed a small recorder and finished the letter on the recorder.

That day my wife Anne sent the letter to my sisters; maybe to bring them some comfort. My sister Verna emailed me back with a word of encouragement, or amusement, or amazement. She used that famous sentence that every author questions, did you write this yourself?

After the funeral, I dictated a couple of other light hearted letters from Mom just for my amusement, and then my greatest supporter, Verna, emailed me with a few words that changed our lives. "I have been thinking about a book...let's do it!"

The sun doesn't rise any morning now that a new letter isn't being dictated inside my head. I HAVE TO get up and write. Most Christians think about spreading the good news of the Gospel, but as we go to our jobs and our chores and attend to our families needs, we may think we're not ministers or missionaries and if I say something the words may not come out right. Well, if you enjoy this book, how about handing a copy to the waitress with a note saying, "For you!" How about the guy that fixes your car, or your hairdresser or the taxi cab driver, or the homeless guy with his cardboard sign. You know, you can't out give God. You can tell them that you know the author; he's a relative, because he's your brother from the family of God.

1 A Letter From
Anne Langeman Klassen

Dear friends, helpers and family

*T*he other day I fell asleep for the last time and my soul was escorted to Paradise by angels. Yes, there really are angels, and a bright light guided us there. It was a most fantastic trip and we were met at the Eastern Gate, at that beautiful entrance of the Promised Land. Many were there to meet me: my husband Dan, my Mom and Dad, and Frieda, Rudy, my brother Pete and my sister Mary, my dear grandson, Clayton and all my friends and relatives that have gone on before. Dan had a brand new body. He picked me up and held me for the longest time; he told me that he missed me, and that he loved me. He said, "Look at yourself" and I realized I had a new body. I was not blind anymore; I could hear everyone clearly. My skin was smooth, my arms and legs were strong; my back had no pain. Dan and I walked into Paradise hand in hand. Oh, what a day that was! We walked in and he introduced me to all his new friends. The angels gave me a robe and crown and they said that Jesus was waiting for me.

We went over to the Great White Throne; it was magnificent. There was my Savior, the King of Kings and Lord of Lords. At His feet was this huge pile of crowns and I took mine off and I put it on top of the pile. I didn't know what I was going to do at that moment, whether I was going to dance for joy or be still and lay down in front of His feet. Then He said, "Anne, I see your name here in the Lamb's Book of Life. Well done, good and faithful servant." He took my hand and then I saw the holes in His palms from the nails. We just walked for a while and He said, "I love you and I have been waiting for you. How do you like your new home?" My Savior said to me that I will never again feel pain and I will never again have a bad day. Just imagine; I walked around God's Heaven with my Lord, sheltered safe in the Hand of my Jesus. I looked down and I saw that the roads were actually paved with gold. He told me there would be no more storms in my life, no more sorrow, no more sadness, no parting, no trouble, just peace in the valley for me and everyone here. Everything He has promised has come true. Everything He said He would do, He has done.

I know you are at...well, what you call my funeral, but I would rather call it my graduation. Thank you to my three daughters for taking such great care of me when I was with you. Verna, Margaret and Janet and all my family-I am so proud of you. I am looking forward to seeing you again here in the Promised Land. You are always in my thoughts and prayers-until we meet again.

It is well; it is well with my soul. God be with you 'til we meet again.

Mom, Grandma and Great Grandma, sister and friend
Anne Langeman Klassen

2 Return Trip

*I*sn't this the oddest thing, just the other day you were looking at me in my coffin and now we're talking by email more than we ever have? You should see my new home. You'd just be blown away. I absolutely LOVE it here. When Jesus said that He was going to prepare a place for us, He really went all out. John 14:3 "And if I go and prepare a place for you, I will come back and take you to be with me that you also may be where I am."

Remember just a little while ago, when you visited me in Denver, and we were talking about Bible characters and Heaven and you were joking about a guy named Lazarus? You're not going to believe this...here's what happened. Two weeks ago Thursday, Dan's playing golf with Clayton, your Uncle Rudy, Uncle Pete and a two thousand year old Jewish dude named Lazarus. That's actually a fivesome but they've got different rules in Paradise. Clay's about to tee off again because he's away. He's beating the pants off of Dan because Clay's always going for the green and Dan's still playing safe and short of the hazards.

Dan says to Lazarus, "Hey, tell me the story of when you went back to earth, that one never gets old." "Oh ya," says Lazarus. "So I'd just arrived and I'm up here having the time of my life. I've got an eight o'clock tee time for Monday, I got yoga on Tuesday, massage scheduled for Wednesday and I got a surfing trip planned with Moses for Thursday. This angel comes up to me on the sixth green when I'm ready to sink a putt for par and he says to me, 'Hey Lazarus, I've got a job for you.' I says, 'Sure what's up, what do you need?' He says, 'I need you to go back to earth 'cause Jesus is going to raise you from the dead.' I say, 'What are you nuts, are you out of your mind? I've been dead for four days and I'm not going back there!'

17

Next thing I know, wham, I'm back on my death bed. Jesus is saying to me, 'Lazarus, wake up.' I'm feeling my electrodes starting to move again and I'm starting to come alive. I'm back on earth! I've got my old mortgage back which was going to be paid off because of my death claim from my mortgage death insurance. I've got my overdue utility bills. I've got a rotten nine to five job. I've got to go back and explain to a miserable boss why I haven't been to work for four days and my troublesome family is jumping up and down thrilled that I'm alive. Jesus is smiling because he knows what He just did. I'm ticked off! Why me Lord, millions have gone on to the Promised Land and you pick me for this show and tell. My wife says, 'He'll make you famous.' I ask Jesus, 'Let me get this straight, now I got to die again?' He just smiled."

Well, last Friday I had just moved in with Dan to our beautiful palatial estate, but Dan had made it into a man cave. See, every Friday it was the boy's poker night and the place reeked because Matthew and Mark were cigar smokers. I was already planning on stripping the flocked wallpaper Dan had installed. I was watching the Heavenly High Lights on the 6 o'clock news and Dan was reading The Beulah Land Times newspaper. There's a knock on the door and I look over to Dan and he's not moving. He yells, "Come on in!" I said, "Dan you never know who it might be." He says,"Who do you think it might be; a burglar? We're in Heaven for crying out loud." I jump up because I've got this new teenage body and I answer the door. I haven't answered a door in years. Here's this tall, dark Jewish Adonis who says, "Hi, you must be Anne. We heard that you had just arrived today and I just wanted to welcome you, but the angels have got a job for you. They need you to go back to earth, get back in your old body and do some unfinished work." I gasped, "What, what, you want me to do what! No! No! No!" I looked around to get some help from Dan and he has the paper up to his face, so just his eyes are showing. The paper is shaking because he's laughing so hard. I turn back to the man and he's laughing too. "Just kidding," he says, "Welcome to Paradise," and he floats away. I exclaim, "That wasn't funny. Dan, who was that guy!" "Ahh, that was just old Lazarus. He does that to all the newbies. Welcome to your new eternity!"

Love ya
Anne Langeman Klassen
P.S. Where will you be the day after the last day of your life?

3 Rocking Chair

*H*i, everybody-here's my new address – corner of 462 Grace Street and 589 Mercy Avenue.

Yesterday, we had a mini-Langeman family reunion at your Oma and Opa's place. I heard they were given a huge palace when Opa first arrived, but Oma just wasn't comfortable with it because the backyard wasn't big enough. So, she had Opa contact ReMax and they traded for a two story brick with a bedroom upstairs, two bedrooms downstairs and a basement big enough to hold the whole Langeman clan. Oma wanted a basement with enough storage room for her baking, especially peppermint cookies. Oma didn't want the upstairs bedroom to have an attic where Harry could hide his shotguns because she didn't want Leonard and Gerry to find them again when those two come over.

She also insisted on a porch that overlooked the street, because she just loves sitting out there and watching who's going by, so she can see who's coming over. Her place is a great meeting place; people stopping over just to sit in the rocking chairs on the porch. Oma always has a pot of borscht on the stove and fresh baked zwiebach and her tasty homemade jam. She now has this huge back yard where she loves tending to her vegetable garden everyday. She has these long rows of strawberries, raspberry bushes, tomatoes, peppers and watermelons. She tells me she never gets tired working in her garden. She told me it feels like Heaven, I said, "Mom, you are in Heaven."

As we all stood in the backyard admiring her garden, I noticed a set of train tracks behind her house and a scaled down train with passenger cars slowly going by, that was loaded with happy squealing children. Ezekiel was at the engine, he always wanted to be a train engineer. I said Oma, tell me about all the children. She lowered her voice and said, "Those are Jesus' special ones." Oma explained that they are the one's that weren't allowed to live. They weren't allowed their full life to experience joy and sadness, peace and turmoil, trouble and triumph. They were deprived of learning first hand about the Savior's forgiveness. I have noticed that the Lord has a special place in His heart for them. In fact, Jesus has a rocking chair just for the little ones and they sit on His lap and He rocks them. He doesn't ever refer to them as fetus, He just calls them His own.

Matthew 19:14 "Jesus said, 'Let the little children come to me, and do not hinder them, for the kingdom of heaven belongs to such as these.'"

Love
Anne Langeman Klassen

4 Angels Singing

*H*ere's one thing I just discovered about angels and singing. The Bible doesn't actually say they sing. It says they "say" praises. So I'm going to leave it as a mystery how good these guys sing but I'll give you hints along the way. You know they try to sing along with us souls-we call ourselves souls. We're not humans because humans have earthly bodies and we don't want those anymore; we have Heavenly bodies. Verna, you should see my new body, you'd be so jealous-but I digress.

Oh, we just went to the praise and worship service last night. All the guys are in the million man male choir. They boomed out one of my favorites, "There is a balm in Gilead that heals a sin sick soul, there is a balm in Gilead that makes the wounded whole." It was in an outdoor amphitheater and it sounded like universal surround sound.

Lilia-I told you I heard men singing, I told you, I told you. You couldn't hear it and I kept on telling you to listen. Lilia, when I was with you and I heard the men's choir, that's when I knew I was leaving. Angelika, you said that I was humming to music during my last days there; well you should hear me now! Tonight we're going to a concert with some angels at Hallelujah Square.

Revelation 5:11-13 Then I looked and heard the voice of many angels, numbering thousands upon thousands, and ten thousand times ten thousand. They encircled the throne and the living creatures and the elders. In a loud voice they sang:

"Worthy is the Lamb, who was slain,

to receive power and wealth and wisdom and strength and honor and glory and praise!"

Then I heard every creature in heaven and on earth and under the earth and on the sea, and all that is in them, singing;

"To him who sits on the throne and to the Lamb be praise and honor and glory and power, for ever and ever!"

Heard ya
Anne Langeman Klassen

5 Surf & Turf

*I*n my lifetime I knew that one of three things would eventually happen to me. If I put my trust in Jesus Christ, when I die, my soul would be with Him and His followers forever. Number two scenario is that if the Lord came back before I die, my soul would leave with Him to enjoy what He had prepared. If I was an unrepentant unbeliever and had refused His offer, I would be separated from Him, and if I told Him I don't believe, won't believe, I'll do it on my own; then I've also made a decision.

Sometimes people go through life thinking that if they decide to follow the Christian path they'll give up too much in life. Well, let me tell you a little life story. A traveler, by the name of Tyler, was taking a train trip when he met a fellow traveler, Gustafson. They were sitting in the dining car, when the waiter came by and asked Tyler if he would like something to drink. "Why yes," he said, "could I please have an ice cold strawberry lemonade?" "And for you Mr. Gustafson?" "Nothing, thank you," was the reply. "Soup for you, sir?" asked the waiter. Tyler said, "I'll have the French onion soup, the tossed salad with honey mustard dressing on the side. I would also like a few medium-sized shrimp and I'll have the surf and turf. And, can I give you my desert selection?" "Yes, certainly," said the waiter. "I would like the chocolate mousse and a French vanilla coffee with a touch of chocolate," Tyler requested. Gustafson said that he wasn't ordering anything.

When Tyler's appetizer arrived, Gustafson reluctantly pulled out from his brown bag a six hour old baloney sandwich with soggy bread, that was warm to the touch, that he had brought along, and then said that he was fine. Gustafson ate and Tyler feasted. When the train pulled into the station, Tyler sipped the last of his coffee and wiped his lip with the cloth napkin and prepared to depart the train. He stood up and was ready to leave when Gustafson said, "Wait, you haven't paid for your meal." Tyler looked at him in amusement and said, "It was included in the trip."

Gustafson was devastated. He had done it his way; he was the one that paid the price.

Love ya
Mom

6 Sweet Cherries and Iced Lemonade

*L*ast Wednesday, my sister Mary and I were over visiting Oma and we were sitting on the back porch swing sipping on some cold lemonade from tall, ice filled glasses. The children's train came by and stopped at the back of Oma's big vegetable garden. The little ones streamed off the train cars and behind them was the King of Kings.

They all walked through the garden laughing and helping themselves to strawberries and raspberries. The Lord was carrying the smallest, gleeful Asian soul and He lifted her up to pick some sweet cherries out of Oma's cherry tree. What a picture that was of the children surrounding Him, holding His hand, stepping in His footprints as He strolled in Oma's freshly tilled soil.

After they ate their fill, they walked back to the train carrying back some of the just picked fresh fruit in Tommy's baseball cap. One of the little boys had picked a watermelon and he and two friends were rolling it back to the train.

As the train started to pull away, He let us know He saw us on the porch swing as He just smiled our way; doesn't get any better than that. Mothers, He sees your grief; your babies are safe with Him.

Hug 'em
Anne Langeman Klassen

7 Beach Day

*L*ast Sunday, Frieda, Rudy, Dan and I went and spent the day at the ocean. Frieda and I were just going to hang out on the beach blankets and Rudy and Dan were going scuba diving. We were going to a place where they can enter the ocean from the beach to go diving. The guys just love diving and they are teaching me how to snorkel. Later on they'll teach me how to dive. It's not like we have to hurry up and learn everything right away. We've only got like-FOREVER! It's the oddest thing thinking that time doesn't matter anymore. There's no waiting for vacation time, no waiting for the weekend to do something.

Frieda and I had the best conversation while the guys were in the water. I asked her what she liked best about Heaven and what she missed about earth. "Well," she said, "let me tell you what I don't miss about earth: doctors, dentists, pain medication, high blood pressure medicine, arthritis medicine, eyeglasses, hearing aids, wheel chairs, crutches, sleepless nights, memory loss and time. Did you notice there are no calendars here, no time constraints? I don't miss hunger or thirst or homelessness. What I love about Heaven is the peace that passes all understanding. The Lord is here; everything that Jesus promised, He has done. We now understand what the trials and tribulations on earth were all about. Looking back from where we are now to where we were then, we now understand that big question we always asked in our prayers. Why Lord, why is this happening to me?"

Looks like the guys are coming out of the water. They've got LOBSTERS! Got to go.

See ya
Anne Langeman Klassen

P.S. Girls, call your brother once in a while. That boy needs all the help he can get.

8 Confirmed

*D*ying was easy; living was tough.

It is almost impossible to comprehend, when you are a teenager, that one day you will not be able to walk or lift most things or hear clearly or that your eyes will go blind. You can't comprehend that you will need constant oxygen from a tank to breathe. As a young person, you don't think that your heart, that allows you to run track, will someday not be able to work well enough to keep you alive. But someday it will. I know that the thought of dying is very scary. When your brain and your heart stop working, do not fear if you know that your soul belongs to the One who made you in the first place. I found that dying was easy; it was living that was tough.

Although I was hard of hearing even with my hearing aids on, my last week on earth I heard a men's choir and I kept on asking, "Lilia, can you hear that, Lilia, can you hear the men singing?" They sang the four part harmony so loud I would call to Lilia, "Come into my bedroom and hear the choir." But she only ever said she couldn't hear them. Angelika had noticed that I was doing something out of the ordinary, I was humming. What she didn't know is that I was humming along with the choir that I was hearing. God was preparing me. The Maker of the universe, the King who had breathed life into this body was preparing me to leave it behind. I was blind, but I could see the bright round light in the corner of the room. Remember, Lilia, I told you about the light. You could have humored me and said, "Oh ya Anne, I see it," but you didn't. But as much as you couldn't see it, I could. In talking to a lot of souls here, it's not an uncommon thing. It's kind of like a big white welcome sign. Really nothing to be alarmed about, it's quite enjoyable.

For weeks before I came here, my living was getting tougher and tougher and then on that final night, Verna came to spend the night with me. Dan and I had lived in this apartment for many years until his graduation and now it was my time. Verna and Margaret saw that I was in distress. The hospice nurse visited in the afternoon, because my new pain challenges were really hard for everybody. I knew that while I was sleeping, Verna was pleading with God to take me to Heaven. I could see that Verna was finally ready to let go and let God. I had asked her previously to let me die in my apartment and not in the hospital. I could hear her pleading to our Heavenly Father.

I had a couple of strokes that morning and there again was that beautiful light. Verna, you laid me in my bed, surrounded by pillows, covered by a light blanket; making me as comfortable as possible. She continued to ask God for relief and He answered her prayers. I observed you when I was elevated in the corner of the room. I was allowed to stay and watch as you tended to my body. I held your hand and you weren't aware when I kissed you for the last time before I departed. I wiped your tears away with my cheek. Margaret, I had the longest hug with you. You are such a wonderful daughters. I was there when the hospice lady came to the apartment and you asked if I was dead. She said, "Confirmed." Confirmed I heard, confirmed.

But, I'll tell you what's CONFIRMED. I confirm that there is a Savior and He loves me. I confirm there is forgiveness and I can live with Him forever. I confirm that the path that was shown to me is available to anyone who asks for it. I confirm that my worst day now is ten thousand times better than my best day on earth. I once was deaf; now I can hear. I once was blind; now I can see.

1 Corinthians 1:4-9 "I always thank God for you because of His grace given you in Christ Jesus. For in Him you have been enriched in every way-in all your speaking

and in all your knowledge-because our testimony about Christ was confirmed in you. Therefore you do not lack any spiritual gift as you eagerly wait for our Lord Jesus Christ to be revealed. He will keep you strong to the end, so that you will be blameless on the day of our Lord Jesus Christ. God, who has called you into fellowship with His Son Jesus Christ our Lord, is faithful."

Life without Him is no life at all
Anne Langeman Klassen
P.S. As a favor to me please call your mother-in-law just to say hi.

9 Mercy

I've been meeting some of the most interesting souls lately. Some of them I didn't even know before, but because of something that Dan or I did, had an effect on their life. As you know, one thing in Dan's life was that he was faithful. You could count on him. His yes, was yes and his no, was no. Well, maybe, except when the girls had spent their allowance and they were cuddling up to him for something extra for the week. Dan was a very disciplined person until then. With a small grin and a twinkle in his eye, he would string them along a bit to make his point, but he would eventually go into his wallet for what he called an advance, but the girls just thought of it as mercy. We have met souls who said they were influenced by Dan because of the way he lived. They watched him, they observed his life. Although Dan didn't preach like Peter and he didn't pray like Paul, you could always say he was faithful for the cause of Christ.

Last week on Friday, we went to a praise and worship meeting and the music was outstanding. Some souls who died thousands of years ago still play the instruments that they grew up with, like the harp and the lyre. I'm getting used to not getting tired or weary and not thinking at the end of the service that I've got to rush home because there's so much to do for tomorrow. Now, I've got endless tomorrows. Time, oh ya, time is the enemy. Think about all the things you do because you are concerned with time. Son, here time is no more; it's called ETERNITY. Jesus told me I will never get old again and I will have all the time to do everything I want and He is offering this to you. Do you want it? Then take it.

The speaker at the praise and worship service was the thief that was crucified along with Jesus. As you might remember, he was a nasty individual. He was the criminal that hung on the cross next to Jesus. Judgment day was there for him and his goose was cooked. He even admitted that it was his fault that he was being punished. Then he looked over and saw what many other people did not see, an innocent man spiked to a cross. He even said, "I'm guilty but you're innocent." He believed that the One dying beside him was the Lamb of God and asked for forgiveness. Jesus, the Great I Am, looked at this condemned man who admitted he deserved what he got and He showed mercy.

Well, I was eagerly waiting for this soul's sermon because I really thought he had a story to tell. When he stood up the crowd hushed. Everyone leaned forward to catch every word from this redeemed soul. He spread his arms as if he was still being crucified on the cross and said just these six words, "FORGIVEN, FORGIVEN, EVEN I WAS FORGIVEN."

Luke 23:42-43 "Then he said, 'Jesus, remember me when You come into your Kingdom.' Jesus answered him, 'I tell you the truth, today you will be with Me in Paradise.'"

Talk to you later.

Love ya
Anne Langeman Klassen
P.S. Torrential rains of mercy brings flowing rivers of grace and waves of forgiveness.

10 Problem Solving

*G*erry, Oma says hi and she gives you a big hug and a kiss. I told her about how you were feeling bad about your weight problem. She advised, "What he should do is have his wife, Anne, bake a cherry pie for him to eat." I asked, "How is that going to solve his problem?" Oma replied, "I thought he was complaining about feeling bad. You can't feel bad and eat a cherry pie at the same time." Just wants to make you say, "Hmmmm!" "But, Oma, he's feeling down about being overweight." "Look," she said, "I just solved one of his two problems, feeling bad and being fat. I just reduced his concerns by half. Let the boy straighten up and figure out the other half of his problems himself. I know one thing, his cousin Leonard wouldn't be bringing me his concerns. He's as skinny as a rail."

Too much to gain to lose
Anne Langeman Klassen

11 Hooey

*W*e were at the Pope's Friday fish fry, when a little redheaded Irish boy with the cutest accent came up to him and asked the Pope to explain a story. "I'll try," said the Pope. The boy goes on, "See, Mr. Pope, two blonde Valley girls from California are walking down the street in Disneyland, when a man approaches them and says, 'Are you two sisters?' 'Da,' the taller blonde says, 'we're not even Catholic.'"

When I was back on earth, I heard this story. Frank, an unbeliever, approached a Christian named Barney and said that the Bible was a bunch of malarkey. "Makes no sense; it's a joke and a waste of time," said Frank, "Prove to me any of that hooey in the Bible makes any sense." Barney didn't say anything. "Well, what's your answer?" said Frank, "Prove to me there is a God and there is a Heaven." Barney said, "I'm waiting." "For what?" Frank asked. Barney answered, "Oh! About one hundred years should do it. Then we'll both know."

See ya
Anne Langeman Klassen

12 The Future

*S*on, I just spent another day in Paradise. No earthly song can be sung that will describe what this day was like. No tongue can describe what He has prepared for you. I am just now putting together a list of Bible verses describing a Christian's future. If you are a follower of Christ, I now live your future. Here it is forever bliss, the absence of evil. Sin does not exist here, turmoil is banned, strife, pain and hurt are no more; new thinking, new minds, as well as new bodies. The Bible says that you will either receive this because of grace and mercy, or you will reject this because of your own stubbornness. He has put in your heart a longing to know Him, He knows you, after all He made you. Psalm 139:14 says "I praise You because I am fearfully and wonderfully made."

If you reject Him, He will not force Paradise on You. I think the absolutely most terrifying words in the Bible are Matthew 25:41 "Then He will say to those on His left, 'Depart from me, You who are cursed, into the eternal fire prepared for the devil and his angels.'" Then you are Satan's, you've got to serve somebody. I plead with you that you don't ever hear those words. Think of the worst place on earth, where evil lives and terror reigns. That's still a place where God does not allow Satan to have full reign. If God tells you that you rejected Him during your life, now He's rejecting you in the after life, the sheer terror that you will feel at that moment should bring chills to your being. Now, it has nothing to do with works. For the Bible tells us in Isaiah 64:6 "All of us have become like one who is unclean, and all our righteous acts are like filthy rags; we all shrivel up like a leaf, and like the wind our sins sweep us away."

You cannot work yourself in, only by grace are you saved and you cannot buy yourself in. Do you think you can bribe Him with His own money? When I died and was laid in my coffin, I didn't bring anything from earth that I owned. No checkbook, no stocks, or bonds, no jewelry box, no earthly possessions, no account of any church donations. He wants us to donate to the church so that when we open our hand to Him, He can put more in. Gerry, He owns it all, and He always will.

When, not if but when, the Great Judgment happens to you and I know it happens, if your name isn't written in the Book of Life you will be forever without His protection. Think of the most evil person who ever lived and what they did to other people. That person was a human and he worked for Satan. Satan is inhuman. He takes delight in hurting you and without Christ, he is your future. In the afterlife you will either be with the one that hates you or be with the One that loves you. My pleading cannot be any stronger. I long to see you again, and He longs to make you His own. I've never met a true, born again Christian that didn't think that was the best decision they ever made in their life.

Please ponder these words from John 3:16-18 "For God so loved the world that He gave His one and only Son, that whoever believes in Him shall not perish but have eternal life. For God did not send His Son into the world to condemn the world, but to save the world through Him. Whoever believes in Him is not condemned, but whoever does not believe stands condemned already because he has not believed in the name of God's one and only Son."

I love you, please accept His gift of love that took Him to the cross for you.

I'm in love with you always
Anne Langeman Klassen

13 Sore Feet

I heard that your wife, Anne's health care provider was cancelling all their policies in California. I was talking to Moses the other day. We call him Mr. Moses, out of a sense of respect or because he's got some pull around here and I asked, "How was it when you were in the wilderness for 40 years, what kind of health care did you have?" He replied, "Lousy. I had a case of plantar fasciitis and every morning I would wake up and my feet would hurt more than when I went to bed. How can your feet hurt more when you haven't walked on them for eight hours?" I asked him, "What kind of health plans do we have around here? I'm new and I'm concerned because my daughter-in-law just lost hers." He looked at me and said, "You got something to write on? Go to the website at www.wedontneednostinkinhealthcare.com." I inputted the website and nothing came up.

Tell your cousin Gary, that Moses leads a wilderness trip but he usually doesn't have many takers to sign up because they're afraid that he wanders too long. I think personally that he's still a little miffed about doing that one mountain excursion alone and coming down and breaking the tablets with the Ten Commandments when his people thought that they could be graded on the curve.

There was a group of us that signed up to go on a zoo trip on Friday and we asked Noah if he wanted to go. He said, "Animals stink." He said he was going to the desert to be by himself for the weekend and I said, "Whatever floats your boat."

Healed
Anne Langeman Klassen

14 Here Comes Trouble

*W*ell, you think you've got problems? Life is tough! But you've got to remember that the God who made a gazillion stars, made the tides to rise and made the birds to care for their young, really cares about you. You may not understand why you are going through the junk that's in your life. When I got here, He told us why, but I'm not going to reveal the secret because they made me "spit shake and pinky swear" that I wouldn't reveal why. But I can tell you when you can't find a solution, you've got a Father who can; when you can't dig yourself out of a hole, you've got a Father who will. When you've had enough sleepless nights and are feeling like a deer in the headlights and you need someone to help you with your burden, you've got a Father who does. Remember, in the end, everything turns out great for a Christian; if it hasn't turned out great, it's not the end.

My Father Cares

Anne Langeman Klassen

P.S. On Monday night, we had a new arrival orientation barbeque with Shadrach, Meschach and Abednego. After all these years these guys still hang around together. It was funny how far away they stayed from the fire pit.

15 Whoo Whoo

*M*y brother, Pete invited us over to his place last Wednesday afternoon for some sushi. He's got an awesome ranch house with acres of woods behind his place, where he's built motorcycle trails through the bush. There is a beautiful calm lake in front of the house. The lake is always crystal clear and it has bulrushes along the side, and a boat rental with fishing gear run by Peter and Mark. There's also a small concession shack that also has bait. The children's train runs on the other side of the lake around the back and through the woods and then right through Pete's huge garage and then around the back of the house. When the kids ride through the garage he rings the bell and all the kids yell, "Whooo, whooo." It also goes through this long dark tunnel and when Pete is the train engineer, he blasts the train's horn when he's going through the blackness and all the kids scream in delight. I didn't know this until today, but Pete was the one that built the train and he is responsible for all the maintenance.

Pete has a twenty foot by forty foot porch in the front of the house and stretched across the two white pillars is a double hammock. He says he often lounges in the hammock and listens to the loons on the lake. On the front porch he also has two custom-made, over-sized wooden rocking chairs that he milled in his workshop. He took the maple from the woods out back. On the back at the top where the headrest is, he's carved PETER on one and IRENE on the other. Irene, he told me over and over how much he loves you and he awaits your arrival and he said as soon as you finish your work there, please come home.

Rocking
Anne Langeman Klassen

16 Reservations Needed

A lot of things are always happening around here. We've got Noah's zoo safari and ocean cruises; Adam and Eve's custom apparel and haberdashery; Peter's ski instruction; Luke's fishing charter emporium(1/2 day, full day, and 3 & 5 day trips); Moses' wilderness trips; and David's sling shot lessons. I give decoupage lessons and the lady at the well runs a drinking water delivery service. Paul is an inspirational and public speaking trainer. Jonah runs a daily whale watching trip. The Pope has his fish fry Fridays. Mary, the mother of Jesus, has her day care service. There's John's sailboat day trips, scuba diving and snorkeling, and surf safaris. The angel Gabriel runs the paragliding and hang gliding school. Oh Gerry, by the way, with your paragliding, like they say, "Break a leg. Oh ya, I guess you already did that."

I've taken up teaching decoupage and eggery and my sister-in-law Mary, has taken up portrait oil painting. One of the things that the little boy souls just love to do is to go to David vs Goliath sling shot school. The boys can sit all day and listen to David tell stories of his life experiences. The old ladies are always telling the little souls, "Careful, you can shoot your eye out with that thing."

Oh, I've go to go, Clayton just pulled up with his new Harley and we're going for a ride.

Working it
Anne Langeman Klassen

17 Stand Down

*D*an's friend, Yytsag and I were having a latte vente half and half with one of the lead angels, Bostock. Those guys really are huge. I still can't understand their ranking, he's a sergeant or admiral or something like that. So I asked him about the crucifixion, what was it like around here then? He said, "Let me tell you what the mood was like. We saw the soldiers approach Him in the garden. When Peter tried to defend Jesus, a fight broke out with one of the soldiers. We saw the traitor Judas sell Jesus out for some coins. We were aware of the kangaroo court where even that little weasel, Pontius Pilate found Him not guilty of anything. 'Crucify Him, crucify Him,' we heard the crowds yell and the judge gave in.

They lashed Him raw and the Holy angels were ready to do battle right then and there and rescue Him. Archangel Michael let out a guttural scream when that soldier came up close and spit in the face of the One who had given him life; it was too much for Michael to take. If the angels were unleashed, the fury of the slaughter on that crucifixion day around the foot of that cross would have been colossal. The Lamb was being slaughtered and thousands of angels were commanded to stand down as they watched their Master volunteer His life. Those soldiers and church leaders and the crowd who took part had no idea that a huge army of angels was being held back by the very One they were torturing. Then it was finished. There will be no defense, because it had to take place that way." He died so that we may live.

Bostock, the angel, continued by telling us that after three days in the grave, an angel was allowed to move the boulder away from the borrowed grave where Jesus was laid. When he moved it, he made a statement. They could have shoved it over just far enough to walk by, but that wasn't good enough for him. He moved it a long way away from the mouth of the tomb. He said to the world, no small group of supporters took and shoved that huge boulder aside. This one angel did that. Hallelujah for that! Jesus left his grave clothes behind and triumphantly walked out of that tomb.

I think I told you that since my eyes are so good now, I've taken up decoupage again. Dan made one of our rooms into my art room and I'm starting to give lessons. I constantly get inquiries from some of the ladies to see if they can join our group. It's a great way to meet new people. I'm not dropping names, but here are some people you might recognize. We've got Ruth signed up, Mary Magdalene, Eve of Adam and Eve fame, the lady at the well, I forgot her name, Esther and Mary, the mother of Jesus.

At the decoupage class, Mary and I were talking about when she and Joseph were having trouble getting a room in Bethlehem. One of the California blondes overheard us and offered that she would have googled travelocity.com and made a reservation and gotten a discount. No one in the room said a thing. Sometimes it's better just to let it go.

John 1:29 "The next day John saw Jesus coming toward him and said, 'Look, the Lamb of God, who takes away the sin of the world!'"

Angels watched
Anne Langeman Klassen
P.S. Dan and I are going to a funeral celebration this Saturday. It's for fear and death...they've both passed away.

18 Something Is Happening

*O*n our ocean cruise, we were relaxing on some lounge chairs and this Roman soldier from two thousand years ago walks up. I just can't get used to the mini skirts these guys wear. We got to talking and he tells us his life story. He introduced himself and said, "Hi, Anne, my name is Angelo. Me and four other soldiers were on crucifixion duty on this Friday. So there were three guys that we were going to crucify that day, Jesus, and two other criminals. Crucifixion day is really tough. Sometimes they don't die right away. We beat Jesus up pretty bad and then to humiliate Him more, we made Him carry His own cross through town and up the walk to Golgotha. He was so wounded that He couldn't go on, so we made this other guy, that was watching, carry the cross the rest of the way. When we say carry it, they carry it.

When we got there, I was the one that pounded the nails through his palms into the cross and I pounded the nails through his feet. He did a strange thing; He volunteered His hands to me which was quite odd, because who does that? The prisoners, who are going to be crucified, fight it to the very end, but He didn't. He acted like a lamb before the slaughter.

We stuck Him up on the cross and I mocked Him. I yelled, 'Well, King of the Jews, since you are God what is God doing hanging from a tree? You are the strangest God I've ever seen. You don't own anything, in fact, we auctioned off most of Your clothes. Now, when I kill You, You won't even own a grave, You have to borrow even that. Come on down and save Yourself. You said You could save others, nonsense, You can't even save Yourself. I was the one who spit in Your face. I pulled Your hair, You didn't cuss. I pushed down a crown of thorns until Your forehead bled, You just closed Your eyes. These Jews, Your people want You dead because You said You were the King of the Jews and You didn't deliver, well You don't look like no King of the Jews to me.'"

Angelo continues saying, "'If You are King and God like You say You are, magically come on down here and I'll bow at Your feet and worship You.' I stood there looking up with my hands on my hips and I barked at Him, 'Well!' Jesus in His agony just looked down at me. And that look shook me a little bit. I didn't like the way that felt. Then Jesus cried, 'My God, my God, why have You forsaken me?' Matthew 27:46 If He is God who is He calling to, His Father? Something's going on here. Then He said, 'It is finished.' John 19:30 and He slumped down. Something's going on.

It was getting late in the day and they weren't dying as scheduled. I had put in my eight hours and I wanted to go home because I was hot and tired. I needed a bath and I was hungry. I'm going to break some legs and finish these guys and go home. I saw that the Jewish guy looked dead so I just took my spear and jammed Him in the side. I said, 'That's done." And then it began. The afternoon sky became eerily black and the ground shook. Something's going on.

I went home that day to my wife and kids. She asked me how my day was and I tried to explain. I stared at her and I said, 'We crucified this Jewish guy and, I've been involved in a lot of crucifixions, but this was different.' She asked, 'How so?' 'Well,' I said, 'this guy gave Himself up, He didn't fight. He allowed us to do whatever we wanted to Him. It was like He actually intended for this to happen. I don't understand it, I've never seen it before. This Jesus actually told one of the other criminals that they would be together in Paradise.' Something's going on.

Later on, I heard that some guards had messed up at the tomb that they were supposed to be protecting. They had put guards in front of the grave and sealed the opening with a huge boulder so no one could steal the body and say, 'See he magically rose from the dead.' Apparently, the guards fell asleep or something and someone came and stole the body. But what I didn't understand is why they would roll the stone that far away. Why didn't they just roll it a few feet away, just enough to get in? Why were His people so concerned about other people believing He was alive again? Didn't make sense. Something's going on.

Then I heard rumors that someone saw Him alive and then another person saw Him alive. Why would these people lie? Why cause a stir for someone who lied to you? He said He would rise again in three days and if He didn't, He made a fool out of you. You wasted years of your life on a fraud. Now five hundred people are saying they saw Him. I've got to find out. Something's going on."

Angelo continued by saying, "The very guy who was in the crowd at the crucifixion that day, the guy who denied three times that he knew Jesus, now admitted that he was a follower. Why, after the man he worshipped was dead and who he was counting on to come back, why was he now preaching about Jesus again? What did he know that I needed to know? I was sure Peter knew that he would suffer for those beliefs. If he wasn't positive about Jesus being alive, what was he doing it for? For the next little while, I watched those disciples and the new believers. When Jesus was preaching for three years, there were only a few believers. But now, people were coming in droves to hear about Him and the plan of salvation. That was His plan all along. Something's going on.

I went, I listened, and I believed. Jesus had a view at the last minute of His life. Raised up high on the cross, He saw a dying world that He loved. A battle was won on

Golgotha's Hill, a victory Christ carries through to Eternity. Death's chains were broken. The grave is conquered; death's stinger has been removed. He had risen from the dead. With that realization, the reasons for His actions were clear to me. He willingly died for me and then He, the Son of God, rose from the dead. I lay prone on the ground and pleaded for forgiveness, for I had killed the Lamb of God."

Luke 23:43 "I tell you the truth, today you will be with me in Paradise."

He is King

Anne Langeman Klassen

P.S. I know He's alive, I've just seen Him and I talked to Him. He told me that the last time I hurt, would be the last time that I would ever hurt.

19 The Sparrow

I was walking through the garden with Jesus early last Thursday morning. For me, early morning is the most pleasant part of the day. The rose petals glistened from the dew and the air was overwhelming in its silence. Jesus and I slowly walked and talked, well more like whispered, not wanting to disturb the quiet. We strolled with our heads down and I inquired, "Why did you find it necessary to leave Heaven and come to earth to die?"

Then I remembered a story I had heard about an unbeliever whose family was begging and pleading for him to come to church with them. "It's Christmas Eve, the snow's falling; there will be great singing; the kids have got poems that they are going to recite, please," she begged. "I'm not a hypocrite," was his response, "Nothing in religion makes any sense. I'm a learned man and until now you've not convinced me one bit."

Later that evening, after his family had left for the service, he was out at the barn checking on the animals, when he heard a continuous thumping from high above. A small sparrow had flown in and was trying to escape. The bird saw the outside through the window and was now constantly attempting to be free, but was just slamming its head against the glass over and over and over again. It would soon die.

He looked in pity at that poor creature and knew if it kept doing what it was doing, it would quickly perish. The window was too far up and even if he could reach it, the sight of a person would just scare the bird. He thought to himself, if only I could become a small bird, if only I could become like that little lost bird, I wouldn't frighten it and I could show it the way to safety. There in that barn

48

he realized that in order for Jesus to save me, He must become like me.

He sees the sparrow fall
Anne Langeman Klassen

20 Little Bites

A group of us, Mennonite grandmothers, were at our quilting klatsch bragging about our families when I told this story about Van, the most beautiful great grandchild in the world. He is the most handsome, smart, witty, charming, athletic great grandson that has ever been born; of all times. Did I say handsome?

This is the story I told them. My daughter-in-law Anne and Gerry, my only son, were babysitting Van one Saturday while one of my favorite grandsons Bryce, who is a skilled nurse and my beautiful and talented grand daughter-in-law, Miranda, did I mention she is a business woman, were on a date night. Jesus gave us great grandchildren so that we wouldn't take ourselves too seriously and they can teach us stuff. I had heard that Van sometimes has a problem eating his meal at dinner time, a problem that obviously my scale busting son doesn't have. Van is a boy whose attention is going in six different directions at once. At dinner time, Anne brought out a regular plate of food for her and her rotund husband Gerry and one for Van. Van's plate had almost nothing on it. He looked inquisitively at the small amount of food and after he sang grace in Spanish, he quickly devoured everything on his plate. "Can I have some more," he asked. "Sure," Anne says and got him another plate of the same amount. He quickly eats that and said again, "Grandma, I'm still hungry." She got him a third plate and that satisfied him. When the parents came home later that night, they asked what all we did and how Van did at dinner. "Fine," Anne says, "he asked for three helpings." Grandparents, don't you just love 'em.

Sometimes when you have trouble starting a routine of daily devotions, you might want to try Van's little bites trick. Just one verse, one bite and that's all you get. We've got a natural thirst and hunger in our hearts for His Word, start with little bites.

Psalm 119:11 "I have hidden Your word in my heart that I might not sin against You."

Get another helping
Anne Langeman Klassen

21 Broken Rule

Early Sunday morning, I was sitting alone in the large swing at the western edge of Jesus' garden. The dawn was just waking up the birds, when my Savior appeared and joined me. We sat for the longest time not speaking, just drinking in the peace and quiet. I was looking away and down and He just said to me, "What is it?" I had refused to broach the subject but I think now was the time. I couldn't look Him in the eye when I forced out the word, "Abortion." Even though He knew it was coming, no words were spoken for the longest time. He asked me to read Psalm 139:13-16 "For You created my inmost being; You knit me together in my mother's womb. I praise You because I am fearfully and wonderfully made; Your works are wonderful, I know that full well. My frame was not hidden from You when I was made in the secret place. When I was woven together in the depths of the earth, Your eyes saw my unformed body. All the days ordained for me were written in Your book before one of them came to be." Jesus, Himself then quoted Jeremiah 1:5 "Before I formed you in the womb I knew you; before you were born I set you apart." Then he took my hand and I held the hand of Grace.

In the distance, the far off clicking of the railroad tracks could be heard. Soon the little souls who had taken the early morning train ride were waving enthusiastically to their best friend. He stretched out His arms as if to gather them all in and then He crossed His arms in front of Himself as if He was giving everyone a giant group hug. There is no crying in Heaven, but that day my cheeks were wet with tears.

Loved
Anne Langeman Klassen

22 Empty Tomb

*T*oday, sitting outside in an outdoor café having some scones and English tea, Opa introduced us to an angel friend. He was by far the happiest angel I have met so far. He was the angel that stayed in the empty tomb waiting for Jesus' followers to come to the grave. I offered him some baked goods and chamomile tea and eagerly asked him to please tell me about that day.

"Well," he said, "I was part of the group at the tomb that day, when one angel rolled away the boulder that covered the mouth of the tomb and he rolled it up the hill. The angel made a statement by doing that, that someone supernatural had done it. Now I stayed there waiting to give the most important announcement that had ever been given. The Old Testament announcement of the future coming was important; but it in itself didn't change everything. The angel Gabriel, that announced to the Virgin Mary that she was pregnant, had a very important announcement; but that in itself didn't change everything. The announcement to the shepherds that El Shaddai had arrived was important; but it didn't change everything. The announcement that Pontius Pilate made, that they could crucify Jesus was important; but it didn't change everything. Jesus said that He was the Son of God who was sent here by His father to live a sinless life, to leave His words and actions with us in the Holy Bible, to volunteer Himself to be tortured, to be horribly tormented on a cross, to die and then to rise again from the dead.

For the longest time, I paced nervously back and forth inside that dark, dank tomb, getting the words just right for the most important statement ever heard in the annals of time. I practiced that announcement over and over and over again, because no announcement had been as important as this one. Can't you hear them, they're just outside, they're asking each other where are the guards, who moved the boulder? Sheepishly they peek inside cupping their hands to their forehead to see inside the dark tomb. I'm standing next to the grave clothes that still have His form. It's time! I savor this moment; the most impactful announcement ever given in human history."

On that resurrection morning the angel said, "Why do you look for the living among the dead? He is not here. HE IS RISEN! HE'S ALIVE!" THAT CHANGED EVERYTHING!

God bless
Anne Langeman Klassen

23 Non-Profit

*Y*esterday, I was taking a stroll with my grandson, Clayton, and we went by a house with a plaque out front-Private Practice Psychiatrist, Family Therapist, Grief Counselor and Financial Planner. We rang the door bell and this handsome, strong, healthy-looking soul answered the door. We introduced ourselves and he told us his name was Job. I forget what his last name was; I've got a good memory but it's short.

I asked him about his life story. He said that we should sit down when I've got some time and he'll tell me all about it. I said, "Not to be nosy, but how many clients would you have every week?" "None," he replies. "How many people needed your help last year?" "None," he said. "Well, how many since you started the service?" "None," he said, "I've been here for twenty-five hundred years and not one soul has needed my help." "How do you cover your expenses if you don't have any clients? How do you pay for this palatial estate?" "It was given to me," he said. "How about the upkeep of the stables, herds of animals, barns, pool and tennis court?" "All included," he said. "How do you pay taxes if you don't have any profit or are you a 501c3?" "I've been a non-profit for twenty-five centuries." "You don't have a problem with the IRS looking over your shoulder?" I asked. "No problem, no taxes," he said.

I asked him, "Job, if you haven't had a client for 2500 years, why do you still have a sign that says you can help with depression?" He replied, "Just think about it!"

Thinking
Anne Langeman Klassen

24 Dead Calm

*D*an was over at the boat ramp on Langeman Lake near your Uncle Pete's house, when he saw Mark and Peter who run the sail boats and fishing tackle store for the grandfathers who go fishing with the little souls. Dan asked, "Mark, weren't you on that boat trip with the other disciples when that storm came up and nearly capsized the boat?" "Ya," he said, "do you want to hear about it?" "Sure," replied Dan.

Mark begins saying, "Well, we had been keeping up a blistering pace with evangelistic services day and night and Jesus was just exhausted. So Jesus said, 'Let's take a break and sail over to the other side of the lake.' 'Okay,' we said and headed out with a group of other boats. We're a distance from shore when this tremendous squall came up and we're being swamped and we're about to capsize, but Jesus is so tired He's fast asleep in the stern of the boat. Man, He was a sound sleeper. We woke Him up and told Him we're not going to make it, we're going to drown. Jesus got up and told us, 'Why don't you believe me yet? I told you we were going to the other shore and when I say I'll do something, consider it done. Don't you guys know me? I've raised the dead; go talk to Lazarus. I healed the deaf; go talk to the deaf guy, he can hear you. I've given sight to the blind man, he can see you coming. See if you can outrun the lame man I healed.' Matthew 8:26 'He replied, 'You of little faith why are you so afraid?' Then He got up and rebuked the wind and the waves, and it was completely calm.'

The men were amazed and asked, 'What kind of man is this? Even the wind and waves obey Him.' Jesus went back to the stern of the boat to sleep, so we raised the sail on the boat and waited for the wind to pick up and we waited and nothing, dead calm. So we broke out the oars and started rowing. I was rowing portside and John was starboard. About a half hour later John's sacroiliac was killing him so he said, 'Hey, why don't you wake up Jesus again and have Him kick up the wind a little bit, so we can sail to the other side?' I said, 'Are you nuts? Not on your life, I don't think He's too happy with us right now. Just shut up and row!'"

Love ya
Anne Langeman Klassen

25 Why Gabriel, Why?

*D*an and Clayton, Rudy, Peter, Opa and about twenty of their friends are all taking their Harley motorcycles and getting ready for the Heavenly Thunder Road trip to the mountains. They all put on their leathers, their dark glasses, polished up their bikes and headed out. The ladies aren't exactly excluded or anything, right, but we decided not to go. It's a guy thing. Besides the girls are having a big pajama party and we're just going to tell stories til dawn. The guys head out in a roar. They start up the mountain on a slight incline and the scenery just gets better and better. They see elk, moose, mountain goats, rabbits and coyote. It takes some getting used to when you can walk up to a mountain lion and pet it and feel no fear. Fear, that's right, that's something that I haven't felt since I got here. There really is no fear. No fear of disappointing God, no fear of sinning, no fear of bad thoughts and bad intentions, no fear of hurting someone's feelings. This really is cool.

There are a couple of grandfathers who took little souls with them and they put them in the side cars of their Harleys. The vibration of the motorcycle and the hum of the road causes them to slump down, close their eyes and doze; it's the sweetest thing to see. The men had driven their hogs hard all day and were half way up the mountain when they pull over for some refreshments. They've got some Jewish brothers riding with them. They don't like riding hogs; they prefer Hondas, but most of the guys think these gliders are more like RV's on two wheels. The guys report back that they've stopped for a while. They say it's to give their motorcycles a rest. Okay, I believe that. They're now around a campfire and telling stories. King David is up. Marcus, the shepherd, was trying to get a brush through his long hair because the wind had it all tangled. The shepherds still like to grow their locks longer than their shoulders. "Why don't you use some detangler conditioner?" Dan asked. Whoops, wrong question. Centurions and shepherds don't use product.

Tarek, the little soul, who was riding in Opa's side car, asked Marcus the shepherd to tell him the manger story again and Marcus said he would be glad to. The men all gathered around the five picnic tables that were outside the concession stand. Marcus began, "I remember that we were guarding the sheep from predators and thieves and were now sitting around the fire; not a particularly demanding task. If you know my co-worker, George, you'd realize it doesn't take a member of Mensa to tend sheep.

What's that light? That's the strangest thing I've ever seen. The angel Gabriel is telling of the birth of God's Son. He hasn't gone to the capital to tell the rulers, he didn't go first to the rich and famous. He's announcing to us. Why did we deserve this? We hadn't done anything. We can't bring great gifts, we didn't give much to the church, we're not on the building committee or the finance committee. We're flat broke. We own nothing and we've been chosen to see the beginning of the greatest story ever told. This was the announcement that the world was waiting for and the angels announced it to us. This must be some mistake."

Marcus continues, "We're to go down to that little village, Bethlehem. I've got some hesitations about this. They could have chosen someone better. Why me Lord? We quietly slipped into the barn. We saw that the little King had a bed in the trough where animals had eaten. The One, who flung the stars into the sky, who set the sun on fire, who counted out the ocean's grains of sand, who made all the animals and who breathed life into Adam and Eve, the Creator of everything was now asleep in the arms of a teenage girl. She smiled softly and handed Him to me. I hesitated; I was about to hold in my hands the Savior of the world. Carefully, I cuddled Him and gently kissed this little baby's cheek. He slept peacefully. His tiny fingers wrapped around mine. I touched the small palm, the palm that would one day be pierced with the sins of the world. I held Him close to my chest so that I could match His breathing breath for breath. I touched His chest to feel His heart beat. OH MY GOD!"

Luke 2:15 "When the angels had left them and gone into Heaven, the shepherds said to one another, 'Let's go to Bethlehem and see this thing that has happened, which the Lord has told us about.'"

For His Glory
Anne Langeman Klassen

26 Smoothies

*T*wenty-four hours a day, seven days a week a cheering section gathers at the Eastern Gate. There's usually about a million and a half souls there constantly singing praise songs. They sing in four part harmony; soprano, alto, tenor and bass. Sometimes they sing old favorites that you might know like "He Hideth My Soul", they sing "Praise God from Whom All Blessings Flow", "Praise Him with Many Crowns, The King Upon the Throne" and many other favorites.

The little souls have the loudest cheering section. Frankie is there almost every day, he's the guy who has the Five Loaves and Two Fishes concession. He also has the best smoothies in Paradise. You can pick different fruits to mix in; I like the mango, cherries, strawberries, raspberries and double dip swirl yogurt with honey. I don't care, I'm never going to get fat and I'm never going to die.

A little soul was there to greet her mother. It was so cute to see her jumping up and down with excitement. When she finally saw her mom she sprinted over to her wailing mother. "It's okay now, mom, it's okay." One of the funniest was when a great grandmother picked up her grown son who had just arrived, twirled him around and around like a little boy. You could hear that man laughing all over Heaven.

He's the song that I can't stop singing
Anne Langeman Klassen

27 I'll Steer

*W*hile the guys were on their motorcycle road trip I was spending last Thursday at Pete's place. Pete just invented and built a riding lawnmower that can pivot around full circle. He's been riding that thing all the time. I've seen in the past when the lawn really didn't need mowing, but he'd be buzzing over it anyway. He won't admit it, but I think he treats it like his lawn go cart. All the guys are always over at his place using his huge collection of tools out of his garage to fix their stuff. Pete is really a neat guy. I just love his laugh. Harry and Pat, he thinks about you all the time and he sends his love.

I strolled down to Langeman Lake to see how the fishing was that morning. A couple of young souls were swimming and jumping off the boat ramp which kind of messed up the fishing for anyone nearby, but there's always tomorrow and the next day and the next day. Mark, the boat rental manager, said to me, "Anne, take one of the canoes out while the lake is still calm and the wind hasn't picked up yet." I said, "Thanks," and went over and grabbed a paddle and a morning coffee. I just love the half French vanilla, half chocolate with whipped cream latte. I also got a sticky bun. Gerry, you know those are the ones that stick to your waist line.

Around the corner came Jesus. "Would you like some company?" He asked. "Oh, thank you, of course, please join me, my good Friend," I said. He grabbed the paddle from the rack and He said, "You paddle, I'll steer." That was a life lesson. Think about it.

We pushed away from the boat ramp and we were paddling around the edge of the lake through the bulrushes, when I asked Him to explain the very important concept of forgiveness. I thanked Him for forgiving my

62

sins. I had asked for forgiveness and He promised in His Word that He would forgive me, but I asked, "Don't You have that in the back of Your mind when we are together? I know when I forgive someone it is in the back of my mind." Jesus said, "I forget." Then He quoted Hebrews 8:12 "For I will forgive their wickedness and will remember their sins no more." And in Isaiah 43:25 "I, even I, am He who blots out your transgressions, for My own sake, and remembers your sins no more." I'm glad He remembered to forget.

Somebody put in an amusing ad in the Beulah Land Times over the weekend. *"Position open for term and whole life insurance salesman. Commission commensurate with policies written. Salesman to pay own expenses. Some travel required. Must have own reliable transport. No calls. Emails only."*

Love ya
Anne Langeman Klassen

28 Later

*W*hen my body was wearing out, warning me that I was not going to be there among friends and family much longer, I could look forward to what's ahead. Now, I've got a new body; a better body, and I get hugs in the arms of the Great Physician. He takes broken and makes it new; He takes damaged and makes it whole. I faced death and you are facing death and some people know that they are facing death sooner than others.

Gerry, just a little while ago you took a trip from San Diego to see me in Denver. The day you were leaving to go back home you turned around at the door and said, "I love you mom, I'll see you later." We both knew what "later" meant. I knew; you knew; and the lover of my soul knew, that the next time we would see each other I would be at my new home with my new body. I can now hear the doorbell, I can now see when I run over to open the front door. So time is short, just trust in the great giver of life and give yourself totally to Him. I'm a living testament to Him keeping His promises. Death has been swallowed up in victory.

1 Corinthians 15:55 "Where, O death, is your victory? Where, O death, is your sting?"

Love ya

Anne Langeman Klassen

P.S. Job was having ice cream cones the other day with some little souls. His favorite flavor is Rocky Road. He says it's a little inside humor. Think about it.

29 Master Builder

$\mathcal{I}$n my small home town of Leamington, Ontario, Canada, a man named Fernando hired a contractor builder, named Mike, to build him a house. Builder Mike carefully drew up the plans, making sure the foundation was strong enough, the walls were thick enough, and the roof was slanted enough. He built a beautiful home. He did a great job and the house was really solid. He finished on time just like he had promised and then he turned over the keys to the delighted owner.

A month later, Builder Mike was driving by Fernando's house when he saw tools on the lawn and some saw-horses on the driveway. His curiosity made him stop to see what Fernando was doing to the house he had built. The front door was open and to Mike's shock, he saw Fernando had the skill saw up against a load bearing wall and he was cutting the studs of the main supporting wall. "What are you doing? You can't do that!" yelled Mike, "You're ruining your house!" Fernando got really upset. "I know what I'm doing," he said. "All my friends said I could do this. I'm changing the way you built it and I'm taking out this wall." "That's your main support wall," said Mike, "without it the house will collapse." Fernando said, "I don't need your help, I don't have to listen to you, and I don't have to follow your rules. Now leave me alone!"

Later that evening, Mike got a call at home. Fernando was in a panic, without the supporting wall his roof was falling in. "Please help me," Fernando begged, "I'm going to lose everything." Mike agreed he would rescue him but he needed three things. He needed Fernando to apologize; He needed him to promise that he would do what he was told; and he needed to tell everyone he knew about how Mike had saved him. Fernando eagerly agreed.

This is one of my Paradise Parables.

Built on solid rock
Anne Langeman Klassen

30 Pass It On

*W*hen I was with you, as with many people, sharing my faith with friends and family was not always easy for me. I thought that it was one of the most private and personal experiences. Do you find the same thing? Since, as you know, I've got a new body, I've also got a new mouth and I've got new vocal cords and a new email. I have no problems expressing my opinion now. Whew! What happened there!

See, now, I've got all the time in the world. Why do people say all the time in the world? In your world, you don't have all the time in the world; you don't have much time at all. We've got all the time, like infinity times infinity. Think about it, everything you do there, you're constrained by time. Everything you do always revolves around the calendar and the clock. If I plan a road trip with somebody whether its next week, next year, or one thousand years from now, no worries, it doesn't matter. Please be assured that you will receive it, too.

At a great grandfather's birthday party, they asked him if he got what he wanted for his birthday and he looked at his grandchildren and said, "NO!" They asked what could we have given you that would have made you happy? He replied, "To stop the hands of time just for a little while."

I just had a thought, how would you like to become an email missionary? If you like my letters, and you like the message, pass it on to ten friends, then ask those ten to pass it on to ten others. Get it! Don't you just love compounding?! Guess who invented it? You may never know the results from doing this, but somebody will, somebody knows and He cares.

Isaiah 55:11 "So is my word that goes out from my mouth: It will not return to me empty, but will accomplish what I desire, and achieve the purpose for which I sent it."

Love ya
Anne Langeman Klassen

31 Whole Life

*T*he newspaper had to pull that life insurance job ad. It seems that Jesus already has it covered. He's working back there with you in the land of turmoil. There are no sales here in Paradise. It seems no one was interested in buying a policy, where nobody was ever going to die. Go figure. Jesus is offering a real sweet deal on the whole life policy. Here's the terms. You're not going to perish but have everlasting life. It doesn't cost you any money, the policy is free. Actually, he owns everything anyway. A funny thing is pockets in a suit of a man in a casket. I certainly would have found it amusing if they had put my purse inside my coffin. Just turn yourself over to the One that made you in the first place. Why not? How good are things working without Him? Tell Him you're sorry for your sins, tell Him you'll follow His teachings in the Holy Bible. He loves you, you'll grow to love Him more and more everyday and you'll give Him everything. No policy application is rejected. The policy will be accepted immediately. The day you ask for your policy, you're covered.

Psalm 145:13 "Your kingdom is an everlasting kingdom, and Your dominion endures through all generations."

I Am Covered
Anne Langeman Klassen

32 Quiet Please!

*W*e have awesome libraries here. There are always thousands of souls lounging around and reading. We've got the library lady who carries around a sign that says "Quiet please". A little soul, Britney, gave her a hug and when she did she stuck a sticker on her back that said "Ignore me". Have I mentioned the forever surround sound praise music that constantly plays here from the Eastern Gate entrance area greeters? It is so beautiful and it never stops. There are all different types of music and souls pick out their favorite songs and they sing along.

Everybody here in Heaven just loves their job and you can switch jobs anytime and you're never afraid of losing your job, because we've got an awesome boss. You'll never lose your job and you're never going to get fired and you're never going to need a sick day. Let me tell you about vacation days, this is nothing but a vacation. I've never had so many friends, stayed up so late at parties or laughed so much. God gave us a sense of humor. I know he did. Here's proof. Get out of the shower, look at a full length mirror and jump up and down...I can hear you now, "Mom, you shouldn't say things like that." Yeah, right, like you haven't done it already.

I've just met a new friend, she's a very sweet soul from Africa and we're going out for a latte and a cruller. Say hi to Natalie & Dave and my little sweethearts, Sydney and Annaliese. Hang on to that last picture Natalie took of them sitting on my lap in my wheelchair. Tell them Great-grandma now has game.

Psalm 126:2-3 "Our mouths were filled with laughter, our tongues with songs of joy. Then it was said among the nations, "The Lord has done great things for them.

The Lord has done great things for us, and we are filled with joy."

Love ya
Anne Langeman Klassen

33 The SHHH Lady

*W*anda, my new African friend, and I just got back with our lattes. We also snuck in a bag of mixed donuts and are passing them around. My favorites are the round ones with the cherry pie filling and the icing. When you eat those, you end up looking like them. We've got to hide them from the SHHH lady. No food is allowed. If we get caught? Well, is it really wrong if you plan on asking for forgiveness rather than permission?

Wanda hears a familiar African praise song from the surround sound and she starts singing along. Listen, her fellow villagers are joining her from every corner of the room. It's fantastic. Every soul, who was reading, is looking up with a smile on their face. Her fellow Africans are now all together in the middle of the room, dancing and holding hands. Their clasped hands go up and down with the music. The crowd was getting into it, too. Nobody's reading; everybody's on their feet. The SHHH lady has given up and now her hands are in the air, too. "Don't hold back," Wanda shouts, "Sing, Sister, sing, sing, sing!" Some of you might think that Heaven will be boring because all you'll do is worship. Well, if this is boring, "Just give me Jesus." The rhythm is picking up louder and louder. Now they're jumping up and down in rhythm praising God with their song. When the music ends, all the village friends hug each other. Oh, look at this, the SHHH lady is back.

I whispered to Wanda, "How do you know all those ladies?" She said, "I had the joy and privilege of bringing them to my Lord and Savior and He rescued them." I asked, "How could you be so effective if you didn't have money and you didn't have a large budget for a missionary program?" "I had an outreach," she replied, "all I ever did was 'Brag on Jesus!' He did the rest."

Psalm 98:4 "Shout for joy to the Lord, all the earth, burst into jubilant song with music."

Love ya
Anne Langeman Klassen

34 Happy

I was teaching Ruth about decoupage last Thursday. You know, almost everyday I have a house full of students. New people every day stop me and ask, "Can I join, have you still got room for more?" I'm meeting so many new souls. This is sweet.

Ruth asked me what I thought of my new home. Gerry, I related to her the story you told me about when your granddaughter, Delaney was just a small child and you took her to your favorite all-you-can-eat buffet. I'm straining not to make a comment about the need for all YOU can eat. She pointed to all her favorite foods on the buffet table as you loaded up her plate. She had finished her meal and numerous samples of desserts, including miniature ice cream cones, with a small bowl of sprinkles, which she constantly dipped her cone into. She could only speak about twenty words at that time. She leaned back in her high chair, put her tiny hands on her bulging stomach and said only one word-HAPPY!

That kinds of sums up heaven for me. HAPPY!

Psalm 19:1 "The heavens declare the glory of God, the skies proclaim the work of His hands."

Til tomorrow
Anne Langeman Klassen

35 Deep Fried Twinkies

I just got a report from the Heavenly Harley riders and they have stopped at a little convenience store about half way up the mountain. Little soul, Timmy, crawled out of the side car while they were moving and was sitting on the gas tank steering Grandpa Grabowski's hogs as they were riding down the road. All Timmy could say was "Cool!" They've stopped at a convenience store and Grandpa Grabowski picked up two root beers, two super-size tootsie rolls, and, look over there, they've got a double dip soft swirl chocolate ice cream cone machine right beside the deep fried twinkie maker. He looked back over his shoulder to Timmy and said, "And what do you want to get?" Grandpas, don't you just love 'em?

How come God made Grandpa's so smart. They can make a sling shot out of a Y in a tree branch and thin slices of an old inner tube. They can read a bed time story slowly and make it interesting. They groan when they get off the floor after playing with their grandkids and they can fall asleep in a chair faster than their grandkids can. They are always dribbling food on their shirt and they don't care. They understand kids jokes and they always laugh with them. And they really listen to kids. It reminds me of how our Heavenly Father cares.

1 Peter 5:6-7 "Humble yourselves, therefore, under God's mighty hand, that He may lift you up in due time. Cast all your anxiety on Him because He cares for you."

And verses 10-11 says, "And the God of all grace, who called you to His eternal glory in Christ, after you have suffered a little while, will Himself restore you and make you strong, firm and steadfast. To Him be the power for ever and ever. Amen."

He restored me; He keeps His promises.

Anne Langeman Klassen

P.S. My arm is black and blue because I keep pinching myself to see if this is real. Will things be this much fun for ever and ever? I asked Adam and Eve and they said, "So far, so good."

36 The Dictionary

I went to the library last Monday afternoon and Wanda was sitting there with some of her friends. I didn't approach her, well you know, sometimes you get a little apprehensive, you don't know who the people are and you don't know their personalities and you don't know if they'll talk about you behind your back. But then I think, no, that was the old being. The new being is altogether different. No back biting, no sly comments, no dissing each other. The reason is, there is no evil here, no evil one who comes to destroy and twist your thoughts. No curse of sin. I just love it.

So Wanda got up and ran over to me, threw her arms around me and said, "Come over here, Anne, and meet your future best friends." As you know when I was on earth, I wasn't much of an adult hugger, but I just love the new me! She introduced me to all of her friends. They're like a gaggle of saints. I asked, "What are you girls doing today?" One of the ladies was looking over my shoulder. OH, OH, the SHHH lady is heading our way. We quieted down, and they told me that they were looking up in the dictionary the meaning of the words eternity and paradise, to see if they got it right.

The dictionary has eternity as infinite or endless time, the endless time after death. We then looked up paradise and it read, any place or state of great happiness. Then we turned over to Heaven, and it said attained by good after death. I thought WOW, how wrong was that statement. The Bible says in Romans 3:23 "all have sinned and fall short of the glory of God." Matthew 4:17 "From that time on Jesus began to preach, 'Repent, for the kingdom of Heaven is near.'" and Ephesians 2:8 "For it is by grace you have been saved, through faith-and this not from yourselves, it is the gift of God."

Well, I wasn't good. I didn't deserve Heaven for anything that I did. I was welcomed in because of Jesus, who said because you asked Me and apologized for your sins and followed Me, I welcome you to live with Me. How cool is that? He washed me clean and forever and ever I will gratefully praise Him.

Psalm 8:3-5 "When I consider your heavens, the work of your fingers, the moon and the stars, which You have set in place, what is man that you are mindful of him, the son of man that you care for him? You made him a little lower than the heavenly beings and crowned him with glory and honor."

Sister Wanda and the saints say, hi. Hey, that sounds like the name for our new vocal band-"Sister Wanda and the Saints".

Love from my extended family
Anne Langeman Klassen
P.S. Anyone else who sees this letter, please ask for daily guidance for my boy in your daily prayers, he needs it right now.

37 Refiner's Fire

*I*t is the most unimaginable beautiful morning I've seen since I got here. There are unbelievable colors and that fantastic aroma of a new day. You have a constant feeling of bliss here in Heaven, all the time, never any down times. Then, there He is approaching me. I love my time with Him in the morning. He wraps His arms around me and holds me tight for the longest time. He is the reason I breathe. I am overwhelmed by joy and then He says, "Let's talk about it." He knows what's on my mind.

It was about THAT time, back then, back there. The time my son stumbled and fell. He didn't understand how You could forgive that. As You know, for the longest time, he didn't talk to You and when he did, it was to beg and it seemed like You didn't hear him. He was miserable. Depression... it felt like he was being crushed. He just wanted to disappear. He felt separated from You. He was crying in his pillow at two o'clock in the morning. The pain was too much. He felt like nobody else was suffering like he was, and nobody cared. His relationships were suffering, his marriage was suffering. He cried, "This is more than I can take. Jesus, I can't take this pain anymore." He was facing a hill that he couldn't climb. He didn't know how to turn this around. He pleaded for You to see him through that. He needed Your mercy. He pleaded to take that away from him. He was miserable and he felt what hell must be like. Hell is being separated from You. Thinking he was separated from his best friend, his Savior, was hell. He knows now that he had separated himself from You, but You never left him. All along You were carrying him, always there with Your cloud of amazing grace around him. You were there even without him calling. It's You who makes him strong. You didn't cause his depression, but You allowed it. The Great Provider saw that it was necessary for him to lose all the luxuries, so he could gain all the necessities. But just like heat makes steel stronger, You allowed him to be put into the refiner's fire. You saw from the future back to the past and You knew it was going to be for Your glory. I love You. You are the answer to every earthly question. He's not a nobody 'cause You Jesus, made him a "Somebody".

Til tomorrow

Anne Langeman Klassen

P.S. Tears are God's Tenderizer. I saw Jesus today and I mentioned your name.

38 Guaranteed

I read an interesting article explaining some things in earthly real estate. The author, in order to protect himself from lawsuits and liability, said that he was not positive of the truthfulness of the information that he was giving out and that he wasn't responsible if the advice that he was giving was incorrect and you suffered harm. How much confidence do you have in his advice if the author won't stand behind it? He's not taking responsibility for any incorrect statements.

But God guarantees His Book; He puts His stamp on it. Believe it like your life depends on it. It's the only instruction book that doesn't have a disclaimer.

Luke 4:32 "They were amazed at His teaching, because His message had authority."

Lifetime Warranty
Anne Langeman Klassen

39 Old People

I heard Dan and his friend Yystag, talking about a story somebody had told them about a classic car in New York. Let me see if I've got this right. I'm trying to remember how it went. You ever notice at the old classic car shows all the old cars are owned by old guys. That's because old guys like old cars, old dogs, old friends and kids. Senior moments, back rubs, old slippers and kids. Gospel music, quiet mornings, newspapers and kids. Sweet wine, bear hugs, chair naps, and kids. Strong coffee, tea with lemon, senior discounts and kids. Handicap stickers, lots of scattered reading glasses, bold print and kids. Loud TV, comedy, a good woman and kids. Old clothes, favorite sweaters, belly laughs and kids. Quiet prayer, dawn, a good night's sleep and kids. A loving woman, a painless hour, God's promises and kids. Hot tubs, warm pools, a sincere smile and kids. Hearing aids, a soft touch, companionship and kids. A phone call, a letter, slow walks and kids. God's love, His promises, eternity and kids. Respect, freedom, sports and kids. Classics, elevators, foot stools and kids. Warm beds, cool nights, sweet tea and kids. Good food, wide seats, slow driving and kids. Game shows, recliners, old pick-up trucks and kids. Jesus just loves old people; that's why He made so many of them.

You remember that the senior living complex where I stayed the last few years of my life had lots of old people and the seniors were passing away all the time. Poor old seniors, all bent over from arthritis, people who couldn't walk or think real fast. The absolute saddest thing was when somebody died, they didn't announce the death because they thought it would upset us. Like we didn't know we were next. HELLO! Instead of having a celebration going home party with balloons and confetti, they kept it hush hush, like the person never existed. I'm glad we don't do that here. I mean it's a hallelujah celebration. Don't miss this party! Get your reservation stamped! Get on the party bus! Don't be left behind!

Luke 15:32 "But we had to celebrate and be glad, because this brother of yours was dead and is alive again; he was lost and is found."

Love ya
Anne Langeman Klassen
P.S. I didn't get to the classic car story but I'll e-mail about it tomorrow. See, I've got unlimited tomorrows.

40 The Engineer

*U*ystag told Dan this story about a friend of his in a suburb of New York. Robert DeMarco had the hood up on his classic 1957 Chevy Belaire candy apple red convertible. It had the original 283 cubic inch motor with a 2 barrel carburetor and a 3-speed manual transmission. He was trying to fix the carburetor, and was not having any success.

His retired neighbor from across the street, George Strathroy, saw him and came over just to talk, because he just loved that car. He told Robert that he had retired from GM and he was the engineer who designed that particular carburetor. Robert gave no reply. He had his head buried under the hood. George offered to give him advice about what to do to make that carburetor run perfectly. Robert said, "No thanks. I've got it covered and I'll figure it out myself." Robert thought he was the man and he didn't need anybody to tell him how to fix his carburetor problem. He didn't need any engineer to tell him what to do, but pride comes before the fall.

George went back home and rummaged through his old books in the attic, until he found the manual that he had written. It was titled "Repair and Assembly of a 2 Barrel Carburetor for a 1957 Chevrolet 283 Cubic Inch Engine". He went back and said, "Here's the manual that I wrote, it will simply explain how to fix that carb." He got no answer. "Okay," George said, "I'll just leave it on the top of the car." He waited for a reply that didn't come. Robert reassembled it the best he could but it didn't start. He took it off the motor again, took it apart, readjusted some things and reinstalled it again and turned the motor over and over until the battery went dead. Things were getting worse as the night went on.

George saw a mechanic night light now hanging from the open hood, from across the street, as he watched Robert's frustration from his front window. "If he would only accept my help," George said, "I know exactly what he's doing wrong. It will never work the way he's doing it. The carburetor was never designed to work like that. I should know, I designed it." He saw his manual was still on the top of the car. It's sad being here and Robert not willing to accept my help. He could be out with his sweetheart taking a drive with the top down, instead of throwing the tools around the garage in frustration. But, that's a life lesson.

Proverbs 1:7 "The fear of the Lord is the beginning of knowledge, but fools despise wisdom and discipline."

Classic
Anne Langeman Klassen

41 Salty Peanuts

*W*hen I lived in Colorado, Dan and I took a train trip. The click of the train tracks had everyone in a very relaxed mood. The passenger car was nearly full and the afternoon sun was streaming through the side windows. The passengers were either reading, dozing or carrying on a conversation with their fellow passengers. A mature gentleman, everyone knew as Mr. Farley, worked on the train as a food concessionaire. With his experience, he knew something about just about everything and he knew about customer service. Most of all, he was an expert on people, because most of his life was dedicated to his passengers and he learned a thing or two about public relations.

Mr. Farley slowly walked down the aisle and handed every other person a napkin with three or four peanuts; just a taste. Because one of two people had been given a few peanuts, they felt obligated to share. A few minutes later, he returned with bags of hot peanuts for sale. Sales were brisk. Often the one, who received a peanut from their companion, would return the favor by purchasing peanuts for both. It wasn't too long before he returned with his ice cold soft drinks and because he sold the extra, extra salty peanuts, everyone needed a drink. Then, of course, he returned with ice cream cones. Business was brisk.

Could we use Mr. Farley's technique to maybe heal old wounds? Maybe just a touch to someone we haven't talked to in a long time, maybe just a hand-written note with a personal signature to say you had been thinking of them, or maybe a word of encouragement, or maybe send one of these letters with, maybe, a coffee gift card.

Hebrews 3:13 "But encourage one another daily, as long as it is called Today, so that none of you may be hardened by sin's deceitfulness."

Hebrews 10:25 "Let us not give up meeting together, as some are in the habit of doing, but let us encourage one another-and all the more as you see the Day approaching."

Just a touch
Anne Langeman Klassen

42 Fore

*W*hen we were back there, Dan enjoyed his daily golf game. He had a senior friend, Jeremy, that he would tee off with every weekday morning at nine sharp. One day Jeremy, didn't show up so old Bubba said he'd be glad to play with Dan. Dan said to Bubba that his eyes were really bad and Bubba would have to watch where his ball landed. "Sure," says Bubba, "I've got eyes like an eagle. " Dan teed off and Bubba said he saw exactly where the ball landed. After Bubba teed off, they started walking down the fairway and they got about half way down the fairway and Dan said, "Okay, where's the ball?" Bubba had a quizzical look on his face. "What ball?"

Clayton and Dan went to the Heavenly Lifters gym and pumped iron today. Dan's got quite a physique now. He's really bulked up. We're not vain here, but he sometimes does a body builder pose in front of the mirror. "Look at these guns, Anne, just look at these guns." "Oh my, oh my!"

Love always
Anne Langeman Klassen
P.S. It was just another fabulous day in Paradise.

43 Freedom

*G*erry, years ago, when I was on earth, I heard this story about how to catch a wild monkey in the jungle. The hunters would take a glass jar with a large opening, just large enough for the monkey to slide his hand into the jar. They would put food into the jar and when the monkey slides his hand in and grabs a handful of food, the hunters would walk right up to the wild monkey and catch him. The monkey couldn't pull his fist out of the jar as long as he holds onto the food. He needs to let go of the food and slide his hand out of the jar and he will be free to escape, but his desire for a small amount of food stops him from keeping his freedom.

Kind of like life. Makes you want to go Hmmm.

Mark 8:36 "What good is it for a man to gain the whole world, yet forfeit his soul?"

Just Let Go
Anne Langeman Klassen

44 Unclean

*G*erry, Sister Wanda was telling me about Miriam, a school teacher in her little village in Africa. It was her birthday and the kids were all bringing gifts. Franky's parents owned a flower shop, so he brought flowers; the baker's son, Jeremiah, he brought donuts. Then Paul, the bartender's boy, handed her a box which was wet on the bottom. Miriam sniffed cautiously at the box and asked, "Paul, is it scotch?" "No," Paul says, "it's a puppy."

I heard this story when I was back there on earth. A Hindu, a rabbi named Barry and a lawyer named Mike were travelling together down a dusty road. They needed a place to stay the night, so they stopped at a farmer's house and asked, "Have you got a place where we can sleep?" The farmer said, "Ya, but I can only put up two of you in the house and one has to sleep in the barn." Then the Hindu said, "I'll sleep in the barn." But a few minutes later there's a knock on the door and the Hindu says, "I can't sleep in there, there's a cow in the barn." Barry, the rabbi said, "Okay, I'll sleep in the barn," but a few minutes later Barry was back knocking on the door. "There's a pig in there," he complained, "I can't sleep with an unclean animal." "All right, you cry babies," said Mike, the lawyer, "I'll sleep in the barn." Soon there was another knock on the door and there stood the cow and the pig.

We're going out for smoothies.

Later
Anne Langeman Klassen

45 The Spa

*E*ve, of Adam and Eve fame, just started in my decoupage classes. What a neat lady! Adam dropped her off this morning. He's the original great-grandfather of us all, so everybody jokingly refers to him as Gramps. The custom apparel and haberdashery shop that they run keeps them really busy. He's now added a custom robe manufacturing and tailoring and he's taking on some more help, so he won't be as busy. It's not like everybody around here puts in their full forty hours, you know. There is a lot of slacking off but, hey, it's not like we're under any time constraints and the benefits are great. We were programmed to be busy. Working and designing and building things is in God's nature and we are built in the image of God. The Bible even says that we will work six days and one day we shall rest. We were built for work, that's when we are the happiest.

There was an incident with little Van one Sunday that I told Eve about, that was just like a mini Garden of Eden. This is a true story; no parable. You spent the day with Van at the zoo. You, Anne and Van had a fabulous time at the San Diego Zoo; just the three of you. You took a sky bucket ride over the whole of the zoo so you could see what a beautiful area it was. They dropped you off at the far end of the zoo at the polar bear exhibit. The bears weren't doing much in the midmorning sun, but what magnificent creatures they are. Then you went to the sea lion show. As Van is apt to do, he took the initiative and walked right up to one of the ladies that worked there and asked her what time the show started. Because of his boldness, she approached him a few minutes later and asked if he would like to be in the show. He was selected to pet, feed and get a kiss on the cheek from a huge sea lion. Everybody applauded and they gave him a souvenir handkerchief on which he wiped his hands after handling the squid that he fed to the sea lion. He wore that handkerchief around his neck until later on, when the squid smell got to be too much.

Later, you stopped at California's own In 'N Out Burgers for a burger, French fries, never frozen of course, and a huge delicious chocolate shake. It was funny, on the way to the burger place, Van fell asleep and you and Anne had a little nap in the parking lot waiting for Van to wake up. Isn't it funny how grandparents are a lot like their grandkids. Van is sleeping in the back seat and Grandpa is snoring in the front seat.

After the burgers, shakes and fries, you went back to your condo complex for a swim. The afternoon was perfect; you were all playing in the pool having a great time, when Van got it in his head that he was going into the hot tub. You said no, because the rules were that you had to be an adult to go in the hot tub. Nothing that Van was told was going to persuade him that he wasn't allowed to do it. Even the threat of leaving the pool area didn't stop him from insisting and complaining that you weren't fair and because he wanted it, he should be allowed to have it. When I told Eve the story she shook her head and said sounded like a story she once was involved in.

Genesis 5:1-2 "When God created man, He made him in the likeness of God. He created them male and female and blessed them."

Genesis 2:15-17 "The Lord God took the man and put him in the Garden of Eden to work it and take care of it. And the Lord commanded the man, 'You are free to eat from the tree in the garden; but you must not eat from the tree of the knowledge of good and evil, for when you eat of it you will surely die.'"

Human Nature
Anne Langeman Klassen

46 Rocks Cry Out

I like writing to you every day and telling you what's going on here. I miss you terribly, but if it means that I would have to go back there to see you, well, I guess I'll just keep on missing you son. Eve is sewing me a new wedding dress. I'll tell you why later. She told me I should put all these letters together for a book, hey, why don't you do it? I'm going to send you a list of Bible verses that predicted what it was going to be like here in Heaven. They were dead on. Dead on, get it.

Children on earth often ask about their animals that have died and wonder whether they will see them again. Some adults don't even believe that there will be animals in Heaven. Well, check this out, There's proof in the Bible. Revelation 5:13 says, "Then I heard every creature in Heaven and on earth and under the earth and on the sea and all that is in them, singing: 'To Him who sits on the throne and to the Lamb be praise and honor and glory and power, for ever and ever!" Well, kids who have lost an animal, look at the first part of that verse, that every creature was heard and they sing praises to God in heaven. They sing, can you imagine a singing golden retriever, why not? Have you ever heard the song of a whale or a bird singing, well, who made them sing in the first place?

Gerry, your problem is lack of faith, stretch your imagination about what God can do. If He wants animals to sing, then they start warming up their vocal cords 'cause they're busting out in song. I've personally found that eagles are into opera, bears are into bass solos, whales like more Eskimo-type songs, elephants are southern gospel fans, primates like a good drum solo, deer like an Irish lilt, burros like Mexican, lizards like reggae, parrots like light classical, marsupials are into the philharmonic, koala bears like easy listening, monkeys are into swing, polar bears float to jazz, giraffes swing their necks to contemporary, classic country is the mule's favorite; but, true country fans are the quarter-horses. Kittens are amused by toddler tunes, stage and screen are favorites of the platypus. Party favorites are enjoyed by tigers, solid gold rock oldies are the budgies favorite, soft rock is the cheetahs choice and hard rock is what the zebras enjoy, and you can watch the fish light up when the soul music is turned on. You think I might be over the top, well check out this Bible verse. Luke 19:39-40 "Some of the Pharisees in the crowd said to Jesus, 'Teacher, rebuke your disciples!' 'I tell you,' He replied, 'if they keep quiet, even the stones will cry out.'" You see, if we won't praise Him then the rocks will.

Genesis 1:21 "So God created the great creatures of the sea and every living and moving thing with which the water teems, according to their kinds, and every winged bird according to its kind. And God saw that it was good. God blessed them." Vs. 27 "So God created man in His own image."

And kids, you're worried about never seeing your pet again; well I can't give you all of Heaven's secrets but just believe this, God's got you covered. Kids, you won't be disappointed. God created the Garden of Eden, the light, the water, the stars, the oceans and mountains and animals and man and He said it was good. Well, good we got again. This is like a rejuvenated Garden of Eden without the devil. He's not at this party.

Every Living Thing
Anne Langeman Klassen

47 Lady at the Well

*I*t was early Tuesday morning and there was a knock on our door and in came Alice delivering her drinking water. She has this great home delivery service of delicious drinking water and she also has water in which she adds just a touch of fruit juice to taste. I didn't know this before, but she gets the fruit from your Oma's garden. She adds a little cherry juice and she calls that drink faith, the strawberry drink is called hope and the peach drink, which is my favorite, is called love. I asked her if she could take a minute and tell me what happened that day at the well, but if she didn't have time I would understand.

"No problem," she said, "I'd love to tell you about the most important day of my life. Besides, if I'm late for my deliveries and nobody's home, I just go inside and drop the water off, because nobody has locks on their doors. Don't need 'em. It takes a while to get used to that. Back in my day, Jacob's water well was a very important place, a spot to meet your neighbors and get your daily supply of water. I was there drawing water one day, when a Jewish man approached me and started to talk to me like He knew me. 'Will you give me a drink?' He asked. Well, that was quite unusual because I was not Jewish, I was a Samaritan, and usually a Jew wouldn't talk to a Samaritan, especially a strange woman who was alone. He told me personal things that only my closest friends would know, but I had never met Him before. Who is this man? He told me that I had been married five times and the person I was now with, was not my husband. How did He know? He told me that I was trying to quench my thirst for a better life with unsatisfactory human companionship and how, if I drank the water that He would give me, I would never want those unhealthy things again and He would quench my thirst forever. He told me He could give me water and I would never thirst again."

John 4:13 "Everyone who drinks this water will be thirsty again, but whoever drinks the water I give him will never thirst. Indeed, the water I give him will become in him a spring of water welling up to eternal life."

Then she began to sing in a low alto voice:
"I was there at the well in the heat of the day
When the Jewish Messiah was heard to say,
You are thirsting for things that will not satisfy,
Drink from My well that never will run dry."

Quenched
Anne Langeman Klassen

48 Reap and Sow

I was in the library reading and I came across this story in the Bible. It takes place after the disciples had gone into town and brought back food and they saw Jesus at the well talking to the Samaritan woman. The woman at the well had gone back to town and said to everyone, "Come and see a man who told me everything I ever did." They came out of the town and were heading toward Jesus. The apostles knew that Jesus must be hungry and they told him, "Rabbi, eat something." His reply was that he had food to eat that they knew nothing about.

The disciples wondered if somebody had brought Jesus some food but He answered, "My food," said Jesus, "is to do the will of Him who sent Me and to finish His work. Do you not say, 'Four months more and then the harvest?' I tell you, open your eyes and look at the fields! They are ripe for harvest. Even now the reaper draws his wages, even now he harvests the crop for eternal life, so that the sower and the reaper may be glad together. Thus the saying 'One sows and another reaps' is true. I sent you to reap what you have not worked for. Others have done the hard work, and you have reaped the benefits of their labor.'" John 4:34-38

Gerry, one sows and another reaps, this kind of fits the scenario of you and I.

Reap
Anne Langeman Klassen

49 Leaving

*W*e use expressions when someone dies. We use the words he's dead, passed away, or maybe deceased. Well, my old body is dead but I'm sure not dead. We use the word passed away. Yeah, and you should see where I went when I passed away. It looks like home, my home, where I will never be homesick again. I did a lot of travel on earth with Dan and it was always good to come back home. You should see what our travel itinerary looks like now. Even though there was work to be done around our earthly house when we got back from a trip, it always felt good to be back home. Can you imagine coming home to Heaven where evil and strife does not exist? We don't have locks on our home. When I was old and my death was imminent, just a few short breaths away, I still couldn't comprehend what it was going to be like, but there's this verse in 1 Corinthians 2:9 "No eye has seen, no ear has heard, no mind has conceived what God has prepared for those who love Him."

Now, I've seen a lot of things on earth, I've been to a lot of places; the great mountains of Colorado, the beautiful desert where we lived in Palm Springs California, the beautiful ocean of the Caribbean where you lived. God loves color, He loves artistry, after all look at what He's created. But I've never seen anything like where I live now. Earth was a taste of Heaven. A sunrise in the desert was a taste; a snorkel over the beautiful ocean reef with the fascinating colors of the corals and fantastic reef fish was a taste; a sunset on snow covered mountains was just incredible but it was like a one dimensional picture in a travel brochure. This is the real deal. The thing about those other places, it wasn't my permanent home. Here everyday just gets better and better. Now I'm settled in.

An odd thing about my new neighborhood is that there are no police, there is no need. Imagine a place where there is no crime, nobody hurts anyone else; everyone is considerate of everybody else. That's because the evil one doesn't live here, he has no place in Heaven. He can't reach you to torment your mind or your body. He can't influence you. The reason for all of this is that your best friend's desire for you is that you love Him, so He can save your soul and share His home with you. Don't pass up this opportunity. This is the best deal anyone has ever offered you.

In the House of the Lord Forever
Anne Langeman Klassen

50 Molded

*S*ome parents may not have given their children praise and the kids may have thought themselves a bust, but Jesus says you are praiseworthy. Your brothers and sisters may not think much of you because of your failures and defeats, but Jesus the comforter, says you are a success. Your co-workers may think that your struggles make you a washout, but Jesus, your Messiah, says you are a hero. Just talk to your Heavenly Father, He's the best family you'll ever have. He'll never desert you, everything He does is for your good and He's your greatest supporter. You look back at your assets and your debt and you think you're stuck and you can't get ahead and you figure what's the use, but your friend Jesus, says you're not a nobody, you're a somebody.

I know what happened to you Gerry, when your closets were emptied and your cupboards were made bare, it was for a reason. You didn't like going through that. It was like an awful hornet sting, but the One who sees the future knew what was best for you, and He was right, wasn't He? He needed you soft and pliable and too many things in your life were interfering with what His plans were for you. He needs pliable clay and you were a hard stubborn vessel. So He allowed you to be broken and melted down and molded into what He could use.

Isaiah 45:9 "Does the clay say to the potter, 'What are you making?'"

Isaiah 64:8 "Yet, O Lord, You are our Father. We are the clay, and You are the potter; we are all the work of Your hand."

Pliable
Anne Langeman Klassen

51 Pleasure

*W*hat I observed, when I was with you was that if people didn't think that God cares about people, then they didn't care about other people. If they thought that God doesn't care about animals, then they didn't care about animals. But God doesn't make mistakes and He never has. When He made people, that wasn't a mistake. It was sin that changed everything. I look the way I do now for a reason. He is the maker of me. He made me to enjoy pleasure, eating, drinking, friends, competition, sports, relationships, music, physical touches, loving friends and relatives. The devil corrupted things on earth. Name one thing that the enemy has ever made. All he did was to pervert the pleasurable things that God has given us. Satan never created anything but pain, suffering and misery.

God made His creation perfect. On earth, God became a human form, became a man named Jesus Christ and took on a human body, took on the sin of the world, allowed Himself to be killed for us, and rose on the third day as a physical being who could eat, walk, talk and even allowed Thomas to touch the hole in His pierced side. Some people may wonder what we will look like in Heaven, will we be a spirit without form? Well, I'm not just a spirit, and I'm not a puff. I have form.

We as frail humans put restrictions on God. How small is an atom, how far away is a star that is a million light years away, how hot is the sun? In the Bible when it says there's a gate at Heaven. Yup, there's a gate at Heaven. When God says we'll feast in Heaven; mmmm, we will feast in Heaven. When he says we will have a new body, that's exactly what I got.

Talk to you later
Anne Langeman Klassen

52 I Am

I just heard that you're collecting all my letters and putting them in a book. Well, that's good because I just started a new job besides the decoupage classes. I'm doing interviews for the Beulah Land Times newspaper with famous Bible characters and I do mean they are characters. Isn't it great that all of us are a little bit different? Dan always says that if two people are exactly the same, one of them is unnecessary. You know, here in Heaven we still have our own individual personalities and I'm glad for it.

Oh, about my interview job, I contacted a whole bunch of souls. I've lined up Adam and Eve, because she's in my decoupage class. I've got Alice, the lady at the well; she delivers drinking water to our house. I've got an appointment to interview Moses, Job and Solomon. Old wise soul, Solomon has some thoughts on the Church and State controversy. He's is very opinionated, he'll tell you what he thinks. I've just done a nice long interview with Mary, the mother of Jesus, and I'm just finishing the first draft. I'll send it to you later. Also, Clayton and I are going back to Job's place. He promised to do a sit down with us if we would bring over some finished decoupage pieces. I think he is the consummate deal maker.

I'm also interviewing Barsuvius, the angel who brought me to the gates the first night. What a sweetheart he is. He says he has the best job in Paradise. He's got a funny personality and a great sense of humor. He quoted Mark Twain who said that if it went by merit, people would stay out of Heaven but your dog would get in. I asked him what name he liked best for Jesus; Holy Lamb of God, Shepherd, Seed of Abraham. He said that he really likes Jesus' description of Himself, I am the great I am.

The Alpha and the Omega, the Beginning and the End. If you are hungry I am the bread of life, you'll never grow hungry; if you are thirsty, I am your living water; when you drink from me, you will never thirst again. If you need a family, I am your Father for I knew you before you were. I am and I will never change.

Revelation 21:6 "He said to me, 'It is done. I am the Alpha and the Omega, the Beginning and the End. To him who is thirsty I will give to drink without cost from the spring of the water of life.'"

Love ya with reporter credentials
Anne Langeman Klassen
P.S. I've got a fitting for my wedding dress scheduled in a week. I know you're just dying to have me tell you about this...later.

54 Went Fishing

*Y*ytsag, Dan's New York friend, is planning on putting a patio on the back of his place. God gave him a beautiful mansion on the far side of Langeman Lake. He just loves to sit in his backyard and watch what's happening on the lake, but there's just a slab out there and he wants part of it enclosed. Now, Yytsag has his, well, quirks shall we call them, but I just love him. I think he pulls out of Dan a part of his personality that Dan wishes would come out. So, Yytsag went to our local lumber yard and there they have a service where they cut lumber to any length. He told the customer service man he needed about thirty-five 2"x4"s. "Well," the service man asked, "how long do you want them?" "Quite a while," answered Yytsag, "I'm building a patio."

I heard of this heart wrencher...A man recalled the best day he ever spent with his dad; just the two of them gone fishing. Just a little boy and his dad, the man remembered that over the decades. Then they looked at the father's journal after his Dad's death and it said, "Went fishing, caught nothing, wasted day."

Matthew 4:19-20 "'Come, follow Me,' Jesus said, 'and I will make you fishers of men.' At once they left their nets and followed Him."

Loving my new home
Anne Langeman Klassen

55 Batter Up

*D*o you remember how I liked to listen to the Denver Rockies baseball games? Well, guess what? I don't just listen to baseball, I don't just watch live baseball, I play baseball. I'm the catcher. I always yell out, "Swing, batter batter, swing," and everybody laughs. I also tap the batter on his heel with my glove as our pitcher is throwing in high and hard. The other team doesn't think that's quite so funny. Opa is in left field, Oma is short stop, brother Pete is right field, Frieda is a cheerleader, Moses likes second base or pitcher, Methuselah covers center field and Ezekiel is third base. Dad's got a little soul friend, Fauntleroy; I don't know why, but everybody just calls him Bubba, he plays first base. We had him in the outfield but he got so distracted out there, he'd be on his hand and knees trying to find four leaf clovers while the game was going on. We've got an angel as a pinch hitter. Man, when he gets a hold of one, believe me it's gone. We call ourselves Ageless Ambassadors.

I know a lot of people think there can't be any sports in Heaven, well, let's think about that. Who invented pleasure but God? Who made us to enjoy pleasure but our Heavenly Father? Gerry, you often told me one of the best times that sticks in your mind was the times in the backyard playing catch with your Dad. Was that good or what? It was about as good as it gets to spend time with your father. Your Heavenly Father does not take away pleasure from you in His backyard, in fact, pleasure is magnified here. Remember at family reunions where the grandparents sat in a chaise and watched while the kids played games or got a baseball game going. Well, up here we once again feel like children. The curse took our joy

105

away on earth, made us old and feeble. Since we aren't under the curse here, it's "batter up".

Mark 10:13-16 "Let the little children come to Me, and do not hinder them, for the kingdom of God belongs to such as these. I tell you the truth, anyone who will not receive the kingdom of God like a little child will never enter it."

Play ball

Anne Langeman Klassen

P.S. No problem with the fast ball but the curve ball gets me tied up in knots. Batting average is a very respectable .365. We record our baseball games and watch them again later on. Just like my earthly life the recording never changes. Life beats death every time.

56 Mr. King David

I was at a campfire sing along on Monday near the boat ramp at Langeman Lake, when Simon Peter's friend King David showed up and he had his lyre with him. Little soul, Sister Brenda ran up to him, jumped up on his lap and whispered, "Mr. King David would you sing me your song, you know Psalm 8?" "I would love to," King David said, "have you got your violin?" Brenda answered, "No, but wait a minute and I'll go and get it." While she was gone, David introduced himself to me. He started telling me some stories while little Brenda was running back to get her violin. I mean this guy's got some stories! I've started bringing a recorder along with me so I can record what people have said and the stories they tell me so I can send them on to you. As you know, I've got a good memory but it's short. Brenda is back with the smallest violin you've ever seen. I asked her where she got it and it seems that David works on old musical instruments at his shop near the Jordan River. The shop is called King David's Custom Instrument Fabrication and Restoration. Like, everybody's got a job.

They take a minute to tune their instruments to each other and then they play in harmony and he sings all of Psalm 8. "O Lord, our Lord, how majestic is Your name in all the earth! You have set your glory above the heavens. From the lips of children and infants You have ordained praise because of Your enemies, to silence the foe and the avenger. When I consider Your Heavens, the work of Your fingers, the moon and the stars, which You have set in place, what is man that You are mindful of him, the son of man that You care for him? You made him a little lower than the heavenly beings and crowned him with glory and honor. You made him ruler over the works of Your hands;

You put everything under his feet: all flocks and herds, and the beasts of the field, the birds of the air, and the fish of the sea, all that swim the paths of the seas. O Lord, our Lord, how majestic is Your name in all the earth!"

In tune
Anne Langeman Klassen

57 Little Princess

*K*ing David and little soul Sister Brenda finished their duet of Psalm 8 to the applause of the group that had gathered around the campfire. It's great, because if someone begins to praise Jesus in song, everybody joins in the worship. Nobody here thinks anything about just going over and visiting a total stranger. Even though you don't know the other person, we are all related in the family of God. That's why we all call each other Brother and Sister.

Little Brenda asks, "Mr. King David, what did it feel like to be a King when you were on earth?" He looked at her and said, "Did you know you are a princess in Heaven?" "I'm not a princess!" she exclaimed. King David responds, "Yes, you are, and I can prove it. See, you are a royal descendant of the King from Jerusalem. He was part of my royal blood line. His blood line was predicted from the beginning of the Old Testament. You can also say that you are related to Abraham, Isaac and Jacob. When you were touched by the blood of Jesus, you became a royal descendant, so you are a princess." "I'm a princess?" she gasped, "I'm a princess!" The walk back home from the lake was something. Whoever called out her name in recognition was greeted with a Queen Elizabeth wave, you know where she holds her forearm straight up and her fingers are slightly cupped pointed skyward and she just swivels her hand back and forth. Oh no, I can see where this is going. Now she wants me to talk to Eve about a custom robe, a pair of elbow-length white gloves and she wants to know where she can get a tiara. Mr. King David, you don't know what you just unleashed.

Love from the King of Kings
Anne Langeman Klassen

Matthew 2:2 "Where is the One who has been born King of the Jews? We saw His star in the east and have come to worship Him."

58 Protector

*D*an and I were at quartet practice late Monday and Barsuvius, one of the angels, that had escorted me after my body had died, was there. I greeted him like a long lost friend. I'd seen him on a number of occasions at different places from across the room and across the park and he always had kind of a knowing look on his face when he saw me. Let me describe what an angel is like. They are always described in the Bible as masculine, they sure aren't wimps. They are extremely strong as said in 2 Peter 2:11 "yet even angels, although they are stronger and more powerful" and the Bible describes people as a little less than the angels. They have the ability to assist and protect people on earth and the Bible says to be careful how you treat that stranger for they may be an angel. Hebrews 13:2 says "Do not forget to entertain strangers, for by so doing some people have entertained angels without knowing it."

I started to tell him what my life was like on earth and he kept saying, "I know, I know." Then I realized he was my personal protector, he had known me all along. Then he asked me a very personal question. He asked, "What does salvation feel like?" You see angels never sin, so they don't need forgiveness. Well, Satan and his angels rebelled and wanted to take God's position, so they were thrown out of Heaven. He was curious what grace felt like. You know, I never thought that's what makes angels and people so different. It's two words, mercy and grace. They've never felt the mercy of being forgiven.

The quartet had finished singing and I saw that Dan was heading over our way. He greeted Barsuvius like an old friend. "So, Dan, you knew each other from before?" I asked. Dan said, "Sure, he and I have known each other since I got here twelve years ago and when he told me he was assisting you, I was happy to hear that." "Dan," I said, "can you go on ahead? I'd like to just spend a little time with my angel and try to figure out some things." "Sure," Dan said, "I'll go with the guys who are going to the *Roll On Jordan Bowling Alley* to roll a few frames. So I'll see you later." Tell little Van not to get scared when he hears thunder. That's just great-grandpa bowling strikes.

Barsuvius and I started walking back home and instead of me interviewing him he started quizzing me. "Tell me, Anne, since angels were created as God's assistants, we, angels, were born without the curse of sin. We don't know what forgiveness feels like. What does it feel like to have mercy and grace?" Wow, what a situation this is. This truly is out of this world. I am walking down the street, in the cool of the evening and when I look down I notice that instead of asphalt, God just used gold. I'm walking home with an angel that I just found out was my protector who was assigned to me, who I had never known, and he just asked me to describe to him the one and only reason that I'm here...Forgiveness. Without the forgiveness of sin, you cannot enter Heaven.

Just then, I think I discovered why angels don't sing the same as souls. They have not felt the despair of sin or the overwhelming relief of forgiveness. They don't have that range of emotions. I told Barsuvius that living apart from God because of sin was like the feeling a child has when they wake up in the night in a dark room all alone and they begin to wail. The longer they are left alone the more the baby cries out for comfort. A quick change and a warm bottle at a 2:00 a.m. feeding and the baby feels comfort, warmth, safety and love. The pure, unconditional love that a parent has for that child right then, feeding their child and rocking in that chair while the whole world sleeps, was given to us as a glimpse of how our Heavenly

Father feels about us. Our 2:00 a.m. wails because of our disobedience and our self-imposed pain are always heard by our Heavenly Father. He longs to be in concert with us and that's what Barsuvuis couldn't understand. Why, what made us humans so stubborn and full of ourselves that we didn't want God's saving grace when we obviously need it? In fact, there is a built-in hole in our hearts that only God can fill. It's like the last piece of a jigsaw puzzle. You see where it needs to go. There is no other spot it can go, and until it's put in place the picture is not complete. Our problem is that humans want to be their own gods.

Barsuvius told me that he was in Heaven when Lucifer wanted to be like God. Lucifer was thrown out of here with many other angels and ever since he has wreaked sin and despair on earth. The earth was created perfect, he messed it up. In the beginning, Adam and Eve were created perfect, but Satan tempted them so they thought they could know as much as God. My life was in constant turmoil because of sin. But when I accepted God's amazing plan of salvation, that's when I received grace and mercy. It didn't mean I was perfect...far from it. It didn't mean I wouldn't sin again, I wish that was the case. But the wave of forgiveness that washed over me, whenever I pleaded for mercy, was what makes you and me so different, Barsuvius. Barsuvius said that he knew what the evil one had in store for anyone who rejected the Father. Lucifer and his angels had bothered me for ninety-two years and I'm now done with him, and I can't imagine what spending eternity under his control would be like. Barsuvius just couldn't understand why anybody would accept that fate. Neither can I Barsuvius, neither can I.

Continually amazed
Anne Langeman Klassen

P.S. On our walk home, we see valuables in yards and front doors wide open. Reminds me of the song sung by the Goodmans...where thieves cannot touch it and it will never need repair.

59 Happy Thanksgiving

I am more vocal about my love for my Savior now than I have ever been in my life. The day that He saved me, He had a plan for my life; He knew these letters would be sent to you. I thought when my body turned back to dust that I wouldn't have a voice to proclaim His love for me. How could I, it didn't make any sense? It's funny how we make plans and Jesus has already planned the future. He's using my voice that supposedly can't speak and a hand that seems like it can't pen a story and a testimony that supposedly has been silenced. Now, I'm penning daily about His glory and how every day He stretches out His arms to envelop anyone who will accept His mercy.

My story is a story of eternal freedom, of eternal thanksgiving. I always looked forward to Thanksgiving time because of my family, the church service, the turkey feast, the family laughter and the grandkids' hugs and kisses. I remember some of my happiest times were when I was holding one of my grandkids. Gerry, every day here is Thanksgiving Day. We feast on worship and unending pure love, kindness, friends and family, and all my Christian brothers and sisters. He's all I need.

Happy Thanksgiving
Anne Langeman Klassen

60 Mountain Top

I've got a letter from Dan about he and his biker buddies. Here's his letter to you son.

Hi Son, how's it going. We're doing awesome. Hey, give the girls big hugs and kisses for me. They call this the after life, that's funny because then you must be living in the before life. You have no idea how much fun this is. I thought I had fun in my retirement, when I look back there is nothing that compares to this. I'm on a motorcycle trip with my buddies, for crying out loud, a motorcycle trip! Me! We just reached the top of the mountain. There's a big flat area that's like a large meadow where we're going to camp out for a while. Rudy made a fire in the fire pit and he told the little souls to go find some straight sticks so that they can roast hot dogs over the fire. Nothing tastes better than hot dogs over an outdoor wood fire. The little ones got side tracked chasing ground squirrels so Rudy reminded them, "We need those sticks, I've got a whole bag of s'mores. "

The view from the top of the mountain was, well, incredible, I was going to say out of this world, but that is kind of redundant, isn't it? There's a puffy cloud cover just below the top of the mountain where we are, so when you look down you see clouds below and when you talk it echoes down the valleys and when you shout it reverberates throughout all of Heaven. It's so beautiful here the guys were saying that they wished that they had invited the ladies along. Have you ever noticed that shared things are more fun than experiencing things alone? Hey, maybe, just maybe, that's why God made people, not to discipline, correct or punish, but to share His creations with us. Maybe on this bike trip we just discovered the answer to the age old human question of "Why am I here?"

The guys want to sing some songs since some of the guys from the male quartet are here. That sounds like a great idea. We've got a couple of angels who with begging eyes are asking can we sing along, too, can we, can we, please….Well, the other guys agree, so we make a deal. The angels can sing with us if they'll pick up the tab at the *Oh for Heaven's Steak Restaurant* on the way back down the mountain and we mean everything – appetizers, steak entrees, the expensive desserts and the tip. They happily agree, course I don't know what kind of per diem these guys work with, maybe we're getting the short end of the stick. I don't care, it doesn't matter.

Willard is a snappy looking angel who wants to sing along with us, but he tells us he's got to hurry back to earth to go and get one of God's saints. Martha is a Russian Christian lady who is dying from cancer. Her ninety-five pound frame has suffered more than enough and today will be her graduation day. She's all packed and ready to go because today is moving day for Martha. Willard said that we should boom a song out to her right now, just to let her know that her day had come. Anne asked if we were the ones she heard just before her graduation. Anne said, "That was you wasn't it, you knew something that I didn't know, you knew when I was coming home?" "Ya," I said, "I knew you were just about on your way and the guys and I thought that you would like a little serenade to help you through the last days." Anne was so thankful, "You mean God had allowed Heaven's choir to sing just FOR ME! He sent an angel escort just FOR ME! He took away all worry and pain just FOR ME, my sin and sorrow is all done away with, just FOR ME. He made a mansion where I will dwell forever, just FOR ME, and I am now surrounded by my family, friends and loved ones just FOR

ME." So I told her that in the early part of June, we drove up to this mountain spot and the guys camped out for a few days and sang to her.

We move right over to the edge of the mountain where the drop off is thousands of feet. Listen, the Grand Canyon is nice, but you should see this. So guys, what do you want to sing to the Russian lady? One of the little souls, Buster says, "Let's sing How Great Thou Art?" Okay, everybody agrees. "Can Mr. Spyder Koop with his low bass voice sing a solo on the first verse and can I sing the second verse?" Buster asked." We all agreed and everyone joined in on the chorus.

How Great Thou Art
O Lord my God, When I in awesome wonder,
Consider all the worlds Thy Hands have made;
I see the stars, I hear the rolling thunder,
Thy power throughout the universe displayed.

Chorus:
Then sings my soul, my Savior God, to Thee,
How great Thou art, How great Thou art.

When through the woods, and forest glades I wander,
And hear the birds sing sweetly in the trees.
When I look down, from lofty mountain grandeur
And see the brook, and feel the gentle breeze.

And when I think, that God, His Son not sparing;
Sent Him to die, I scarce can take it in;
That on the Cross, my burden gladly bearing,
He bled and died to take away my sin.

When Christ shall come, with shout of acclamation,
And take me home, what joy shall fill my heart.

Then I shall bow, in humble adoration,
And then proclaim: "My God, how great Thou art!"

Miss you
Anne Langeman Klassen

61 Curry

*T*oday, little soul Princess Brenda contacted me to see if I wanted to go to Langeman Lake. I said, "Sure, how about mid-day?" "Can I bring Molly?" she asked, "and how about inviting your sister Frieda?" I replied, "Okay, it's a date. I'll pick you up at Jesus' house at noon." The girls live in a house that the Bible describes as having many rooms. John 14:2 In my Father's house are many rooms; if that were not so, I would have told you. I am going there to prepare a place for you. All her friends are there. To me it feels like a great big sorority house at a Christian school with one long continuous party and praise gathering. Brenda loves her voice lessons and she tells me that she's now singing solos. You can often find her at the Eastern Gate singing with the welcoming choir.

I pick her up at noon and I can't believe it, she's found a tiara and she's wearing it. We're going to the beach and she's wearing a tiara. Whatever! If the rest of the day is like it's starting out, this is going to be a hoot. It's not too long before we're at the beach and have laid out our blankets and are telling stories. The lake looks beautiful today and Molly comes up with a great idea. "Let's go water skiing," she says. Of course, Brenda immediately agrees and then I ask myself, did they have this planned all along? "I'm in," Frieda says, so we're packing up and heading for the concession stand to sign up for the ski boat. Friendly Brother Peter is behind the counter and it seems he knows the girls. "Oh, I see you've brought me two more customers," he says. My suspicions are confirmed. "Ya," Brenda replies, "they want to go skiing, do you want to take us out?" "Sure," Peter says, "but we've got to wait just a little while. Mark is out with the boat with some skiers right now, I don't think it'll be too long before he's back."

Molly then says, "I think Sister Anne and Sister Frieda look a little thirsty, can we have a round of lemonades?" "It's on the house," says Peter. I think I hear the ski boat nearing the dock now.

Little sister Brenda excitedly points out that the ski boat is headed back to shore so we gathered all our stuff and head over to the dock. I watch in amusement as the girls run ahead of us and wonder why they are here because they are so young. "C'mon, Miss Anne, hurry Miss Frieda, they're almost here!" To some people they are a memory that brings waves of grief, but here we are enjoying their company. Here they have no more sick days, no more doctors, no more pain. I think Jesus puts in a fade control on little souls' memory so that the mommy thoughts don't come up; that's Jesus' gift to parents and relatives. Just you people are burdened by thought of missing a loved one. We're not under any time or space controls either, when we want to visit someone in another part of Heaven we just think about that person and whoosh, we're there.

The girls have reached the dock and are waving at the passengers in the boat as it is pulling up to the mooring. The ski instructor throws them the bow line and the girls are straining to pull the boat closer to the dock. The pilot is Mark the Apostle. Peter and Mark go way back, they were both apostles of Jesus, a two thousand year friendship. Mark looks good. He spends most of his day on the water so he's got this rich golden tan and a swimmer's physique. Not bad for a guy twenty centuries old. Mark said to Peter, "Hey, I'm taking a break, I'm going to lie on the beach for a while." Peter tells him to just leave the concession stand open and souls can help themselves to whatever they want. When I first hear that I think, "You can't do that!" Then it dawns on me again where I am. It's going to take some time to come to the reality of all this and for all the changes to sink in.

The girls are throwing their stuff in the boat before the other passengers even get out. I look at the passengers expressions thinking I'm going to see annoyance with this, but all I see on their faces is amusement. Some words I might as well forget because they have no meaning here. Words like impatience, agitation, restlessness, anxiety, nervousness, anxiousness, discontent, vexed, estranged, resentful, unsettled, peeved, annoyed, impatient, rattled, and uneasy. I'm just now starting to understand what Heaven is about...take all the junk out of your life, everything that bugs you, everything that you don't want to do, everything that wastes your time, everything that hurts. Eliminate all that, the job you don't like, the daily grind of a commute, the dwindling bank account, the low retirement funds, the car that needs repair, the burdensome mortgage payment on a house that you're upside down on, sickness, your taxes, your high balance credit card, your aches and pains of getting older. Take all that junk out of your life and then take sin and the evil one and toss it to the far side of the solar system and replace all that with a Friend that will never fail, a Father who never scolds, a Protector who loved you so much He proved it by wearing a crown of skin piercing thorns and who allowed His life to be sacrificed for you and then you get a small peek, just a keyhole view of how I'm living today. Jesus said that I couldn't imagine in my mind, I couldn't see with my eyes what He was going to build for me. YOU HAVE NO IDEA!

The other passengers get out of the boat and introduce themselves to us. They are a couple from India. They tell us that they live at 4569 Jericho Road and invite us over tonight for some Indian food. You know, when I think back, I can't recall that I've ever had a meal of original Indian food. I remember on earth, that after a day in the sun, if someone said come on over tonight, I'd say that I'm too tired, I'm going to pass. Here's another word you'll never ever hear in Heaven-tired. Nobody's ever weary; you just don't run out of energy. I mean you can go 24/7 and still feel the same as when you started. Weird, huh!

The girls are already in the boat and little Brenda is behind the wheel. She thinks she's going to steer. Peter says to her, "Don't touch that ignition; I don't want you taking off without us again." We pile all the stuff into the boat and store our snacks and drinks in the cubby holes along the side. "Do you have any life preservers?" The words just got out of my mouth and everyone starts to laugh. Life preservers-get it. "Hey, Peter, what's the name of this boat," Frieda asks. She's been here longer than I have, and she knows she can give him some good old-fashioned ribbing. "Oh, here it is on the stern. *Water Walker*. Weren't you involved with a story about walking on water?" "Look," he says, "one little slip of faith and for two thousand years nobody will let it go." Frieda pats him on the shoulder, "I was just yanking your chain, I know you were good for it." "I know," he says, "that little incident did make me famous though, didn't it? When we get back to the concession shack I'll give you a t-shirt with a picture of me walking on water two feet away from the boat."

Then I asked him when we get back to shore, can you tell me what it was like that day with Jesus on the water. "Sure," he said, "I've got dozens of stories and I've got nothing but time." I told him that I was sending you a daily letter and he thought that was cool and says to say "Hi." I'll try to figure out how to get his autographed t-shirt to you.

Loving Life
Anne Langeman Klassen

62 Ski Rope

*W*e pushed away from the boat dock. With the motor sputtering at idle, the boat slowly moved into open water. Brenda, with one hand resting on the back of the chair and one hand on his knee, stared so intently with her burning brown eyes into Peter's face, that it was hard for him to hold back the chuckle as he looked straight ahead. She just stared at him hoping that he would give the okay without her having to ask. "What?" he asks her. Brenda begs, "Come on, let me steer pleeeeease, Brother Peter. I'll steer good, I promise." "Sure," he says and she leaps onto his lap. He pushes the throttle forward and the bow jumps up and the roar of the engine has everybody sitting down and hanging on. I find that sometimes it is more fun to watch little souls having fun than doing the fun myself. I snapped a picture of her concentrating behind the wheel and I'll see if I can send it to you. "How long have you been here?" I asked the girls. Brenda answers, "I have been here since 975 AD." I ask her, "Do you think you'll ever get older?" "I hope not," she says. Just makes you want to ponder that, doesn't it? Maybe she's right. Who delights more in pleasure than kids? Enjoy where you are in life.

We motor over to the ski area and Frieda encourages me to jump into the water and give it a try. "No way, I'm not first!" I replied. Frieda challenges, "What, don't you have any faith in us?" I reply, "I've got all the faith in the WORLD in you (a little play on words there) but it's my ability that I have no faith in. Frieda, you know I've never done anything like this before. Girls, you want to go first?" "Na," both of them say, "That's okay, Sister Frieda you go first." Their giggles give away that they're planning something. Frieda does an unexpected cannon ball over the side drenching everybody, but it doesn't matter, the warmth of the Savior's glow has us all dry in a matter of minutes. Oh ya, I didn't tell you we don't have the same sun anymore. It doesn't parch, cause sun burns, make you squint, or dry out your skin. We live by Heaven's supernatural glow that comes from Jesus. He's our light, warmth and comfort. Neat, huh? We don't need the sun because we've got the Son!

We hand Frieda two skis. She's treading water and now she's got them on. Her ski tips are sticking straight up and she's ready to go. Look's like she's done this plenty of times since she got here, because I know she never did this on earth. "We'll toss her the rope," Brenda says. Brenda makes a weak attempt at the throw and the rope falls just short of where Frieda is treading water. Now Frieda is paddling forward and she's almost got it. Little Brenda is at the edge of the boat encouraging Frieda to paddle harder and little Molly is crouched down below the side of the ski boat slowly pulling the rope back in. Brenda cups her hands around her mouth encouraging Frieda to paddle harder, Frieda is giving it her best effort but Molly is slowly pulling the rope back in just out of Frieda's reach. Brother Peter is turned in the other direction bent over the steering wheel and howling with laughter. Frieda just caught on and she stopped paddling. We're now all laughing hysterically.

I can't believe my situation. I'm ninety-two earth years old. I feel and look like twenty. I'm on a ski boat with two little tricksters, a two thousand year old apostle, my best friend and sister who is floating in a crystal clear lake and I can't think of one problem that I have, nothing. I've been told by Adam and Eve that it's always been like this and Jesus told me it will always be like this. Just makes this Christian want to jump up and shout "Hallelujah!"

Brenda pulls the rope back in and makes a better toss so that Frieda can get a hold of the handle. Soon, we're ready to go. Frieda's in position, tips of her skis are up, rope between her skis, rope is tight and she nods, she's ready to go. Peter pushes the throttle forward and the powerful motor jumps the bow into the air again. Frieda is up skiing within a few feet and she's got the biggest grin. The little girls are fist pumping and shouting encouragement. Brenda even yells, "You go girl!" then quickly gives a glance to Peter to see if she had gone over the line. The rest of the afternoon was spent with pleasure and laughter. Brenda and Molly skied together crisscrossing back and forth, coming so close to each other they gave each other high five's. I tried it; I'll leave it at that. The girls have a great idea-snow cones-crushed ice with colored flavored syrup. We start heading back to the concession stand and now Molly is steering. I still can't believe this is my life now, and my future.

Great Day in Paradise
Anne Langeman Klassen

63 The Dock

*W*e idle back to the boat dock and Molly is over-steering because the boat is not reacting fast enough to her liking. Peter takes the wheel and shifts into neutral as we come up against the dock. Molly and Brenda jump out of the boat and secure the bow line to the dock cleat. As the girls got out of the boat, they had inadvertently pushed the stern away from the dock. The girls are now bounding down the boat dock toward the concession stand while the stern is getting farther and farther from the dock. Some of the other sailors and fishermen see Peter's situation and are good heartedly teasing him about his boat docking skills. Now the boat is pointed directly to the dock. Peter yells for Molly to come back and pull the stern back to the dock. She runs back and grabs the stern rope just as some of Peter's friends snap some pictures of his docking dilemma and I motioned to them that I needed a copy of that picture.

The girls come out of the concessions with five snow cones that they had helped themselves to. They've also got five foot long hot dogs just dripping with ketchup, mustard, relish and pickles. They also grabbed five funnel cakes with cream cheese icing for us for dessert. They've got child-like grins on their faces, that we've all seen before. Now, I kind of hope Jesus leaves them at that age and who knows maybe He does that; I don't know. They pick out a picnic table and they start passing out their food. "How did you pay for this?" I ask. "Oh, we just put it on Mr. Peter's tab," they said, "he's good for it." I've been meaning to ask how everything gets paid around here. "Well," Frieda says, "we just submit our bills every month to our Great Host and the invoice comes back stamped PAID IN FULL. Neat, huh?" Then Brenda says something that had me staring at her in amusement. She said that if it weren't for the fact that she didn't have any money, she'd be broke.

Okay, Peter will you please tell us the story about you walking on water? "All right," he says, "Here's what happened. The day before, we were at a huge gathering where there were over five thousand men not including the women and children and Jesus was preaching and teaching. Jesus said that the crowds were like sheep without a shepherd. So he was teaching them many things. It was late in the day and we were telling Jesus to send the crowd away to fend for themselves for the evening meal. Now think about this, He gathers the crowd and in our dumb thinking we tell Him to send them away because we can't feed them. Do we ask Him what He wants us to do? No! We try to figure it out ourselves. We saw Him heal the lame, give sight to the blind, raise the dead but with our best thinking figure that it is going to cost us too much to put out a meal for His congregation. Why He just doesn't throw up His hands and give up on us? I have no idea! So this is what He does, check this out. He has a way of making a point, doesn't He? He takes five loaves and two fishes from a little boy. Now here's another point. This food was not donated by a philanthropist who wanted Jesus' thanks. This food came from a young boy and that's all they gathered from the group. Jesus took that food and blessed it. He looked to Heaven while He gave thanks and broke the loaves and fishes. Then He gave them to His disciples to give to the people. He said through His actions, watch how much I love you and what I want to do for you. I think the biggest lesson here is that you can't outgive God. You can donate five loaves and two fishes to feed over five thousand people and get back twelve baskets of food left over.

After that, Jesus told us to get into the boat and go on ahead of Him while he dismissed the crowd. After He left us, He went up to a mountainside to pray. Jesus liked to be by Himself in solitude with His Father, especially after a large gathering and a successful day such as feeding the five thousand. And He knew that we disciples still didn't comprehend, still didn't understand who He was. The crowd wanted to crown Jesus because they got free food and miracles and we disciples said, "So what about the miracles?"

We headed our boat over to the other side of the lake. That night we were straining with the oars because the wind was against us. A storm had come up and we couldn't use our sails. Jesus knew that we were in trouble and at about the fourth watch, which was about 3 o'clock in the morning, Jesus walked past us on the water. We thought He was a ghost or a spirit and Jewish superstition has it that if you see a spirit at night, here comes disaster. So, we are in the midst of a storm in the middle of the night and we think that a death spirit is walking around our boat. Then Jesus said to us, 'Take courage! It is I! Don't be afraid!' Then I said to Jesus, 'Lord if it is you, tell me to come to you on the water.' Jesus replied, 'Come.' So I got out of the boat and started walking on the water. I was doing fine until I became frightened by the wind and huge waves. I lacked faith; I took my eyes off of Him; I got scared and started to go under. I was okay as long as I had my eyes on Him. Faith kept me walking, but fear of the wind overcame faith in Jesus. I cried out 'Lord, save me.' Jesus reached out His hand and caught me. He said to me, 'You of little faith, why did you doubt Me?' Matthew 14:28-31 As soon as we climbed back into the boat the wind stopped. Then everybody in the boat said, 'Truly, You are the Son of God.'

Now, I thought about this. We saw Him perform miracles, healing the sick, giving sight to the blind, he told one lame man, who couldn't walk, to get up and he ran down the street, He made one deaf guy hear immediately by touching his ears. We, just the day before, saw Him feed over five thousand people with five loaves and two fishes and still we didn't believe because our hearts were hardened. That's why when I gave the account to Mark, I didn't include the whole story of Jesus walking on the water, I didn't include my attempt at doing the same thing. I left that out and that's why Frieda was ribbing me about my lack of faith.

Finally, in the boat, Jesus immediately calms the wind and the sea goes dead flat. He could have done that when the storm first started but there was a purpose for that all night test. He knew the storm was coming. In fact, He may have had angels cause the storm. He demonstrated our inadequacies so that we would look to His all encompassing, sufficient grace as our only hope. That was a night I'll never forget."

Half way through that last sentence Brenda slid off her picnic bench and started running for the shore with Molly in hot pursuit. She was running down the slight decline over the grass and down to the sand at the lake's edge. Molly veered off and headed straight for the concession stand where she exited in a matter of seconds with a jumbo cherry snow cone. She ran to the shore bent over holding the drink with two hands in front of her. Brenda got there before her and was greeted by the love of her life. Out of breath Molly yelled, "I got a snow cone for you Jesus!" A little soul had brought her Heavenly Father, the God, who created the universe; she had brought Him an icy snow cone. YES!

Love ya
Anne Langeman Klassen

64 Wedding Dress

I'm going to Eve's place for another fitting of my wedding dress next Thursday. I am so excited for the wedding supper as we celebrate the marriage of the Lamb. I can hardly wait for the celebration to begin, when the groom says, "I've prepared a feast for you, my loved ones, come and dine." I'll wear my brand new wedding dress, so white and clean, as Christ marries His Church and we honor and consecrate the name of the One who is worthy.

Hosea 2:19 "I will betroth you to me forever; I will betroth you in righteousness and justice, in love and compassion. I will betroth you in faithfulness, and you will acknowledge the Lord."

Revelation 19:7-9 "Let us rejoice and be glad and give Him Glory! For the wedding of the Lamb has come, and His bride has made herself ready. Fine linen, bright and clean, was given her to wear... Blessed are those who are invited to the wedding supper of the Lamb!"

Betrothed
Anne Langeman Klassen

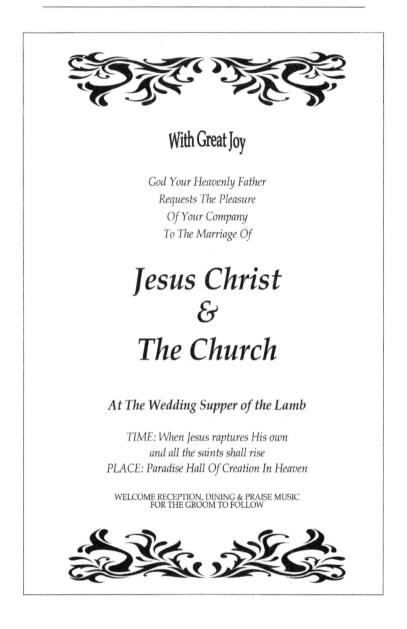

With Great Joy

God Your Heavenly Father
Requests The Pleasure
Of Your Company
To The Marriage Of

Jesus Christ
&
The Church

At The Wedding Supper of the Lamb

TIME: When Jesus raptures His own
and all the saints shall rise
PLACE: Paradise Hall Of Creation In Heaven

WELCOME RECEPTION, DINING & PRAISE MUSIC
FOR THE GROOM TO FOLLOW

65 Perfect Love

Very early Sunday morning, Dan and his quartet, along with two angel friends were practicing their new songs, because they are singing at the Eastern Gate today. The angels are really singing good this morning. They tend to like the faster songs-more upbeat; but Dan kind of leans to the old gospel slower ballads. But to each his own. So they always have a good mix. The guys asked me to sing the soprano part along with Yytsag, who is a baritone. We, sometimes sing duets together, which is kind of nice.

I often walk around Langeman Lake first thing in the morning and it is just a fabulous morning. Because it's so early, nothing much is happening at the concession stand and I see Peter and I wave good morning. I see he's rented a canoe to Brenda and Molly; they're out early and I can hear them giggling. They're both paddling on the same side of the canoe and they'll be paddling in circles all day, but at least they won't get too far from the shore. I wonder how they got to the lake. I walk past the bulrushes, where the frogs are croaking and a couple of turtles are sitting on a partially submerged log. The loons are making their music and a pair of ducks swims in and out of the bulrushes. Suddenly, I feel His presence beside me. "Good morning, Anne," the Master says. "Oh, my precious Lord," I whisper as I curl into His chest as He holds me close. He's got such beautiful eyes and a gaze that you immediately know He is aware of everything that's going on with you. He has talked before about being perfectly loved. THIS is what He was talking about. We walk hand in hand as we both kick pure white sand in front of us.

I gaze across this beautiful lake that we are walking around and view the mountains in the background and I think of the mansion He has given us, the great jobs that I have, the contentment I feel everyday, the reunion with my family, all the great new friends that I have and the joy of spending eternity with them. I think about who I am and question why I deserve what He prepared for me. There is not a thing that I did to deserve this. I brought nothing to Jesus to deserve Heaven. Then I looked down and saw the one thing that I had brought into Heaven: it is the nail prints in my Savior's feet.

Psalm 23:6 "Surely goodness and love will follow me all the days of my life, and I will dwell in the house of the Lord forever."

From across the lake I could hear Brenda playing her violin and Molly singing:

The Love of God
The love of God is greater far
Than tongue or pen can ever tell;
It goes beyond the highest star,
And reaches to the lowest hell;
The guilty pair, bowed down with care,
God gave His Son to win;
His erring child He reconciled,
And pardoned from his sin.
Refrain:
Oh, love of God, how rich and pure!
How measureless and strong!
It shall forevermore endure-
The saints' and angels' song.

Could we with ink the ocean fill,
And were the skies of parchment made,
Were every stalk on earth a quill,
And every man a scribe by trade;
To write the love of God above

Would drain the ocean dry;
Nor could the scroll contain the whole,
Though stretched from sky to sky.

Goodness
Anne Langeman Klassen

66 Paradise Pool and Cue (Part 1 of 6)

My angel, Barsuvius and I had such a great evening talking about angels and their roles since Creation that I asked him if he could introduce me to some of his fellow angels and could I interview them for the Beulah Land Times. He said that the guys were getting together tomorrow night at the *Paradise Pool and Cue*, to have a few friendly games of pool and he would take me there and introduce me to some of his friends. "But here's a warning that Dan, your husband, knows full well," he said, "When the newbies first arrive in Heaven, the angels always introduce themselves and ask if you would like to have a friendly game of pool. They even say since you're new here and you aren't familiar with the tables, they'll even spot you. BEWARE! They've only been practicing pool since the beginning of time. And be real careful of your answer if they ask, 'Hey, why don't we make it interesting and we can play for a few shekels.' If you agree, you might as well sit down 'cause they'll run the table on you. These guys can walk through walls, conquer armies and become invisible. Like you've got a chance at their game...right."

Barsuvius brought me into the game room and we are immediately approached by this huge handsome supernatural being. He said, "Hi, my name is Robert and what is your name?" I reply, "Anne." "Would you like to have a friendly game of pool?" he inquires. Then Barsuvius interrupted saying, "Forget it, Robert, I already warned her." "Oh come on," he says, "just for sport, nothing else. It's kind of like an angelic initiation." "Sure," I said, "but I work for the Beulah Land Times, so can I interview you while we play?" "Sure," he says, "Eight ball okay with you?" "Sure,"

I said, "but what is eight ball?" "I'll rack 'em...you break," he said, "I'll teach you."

Then I said, "Until a little while ago, I didn't know very much about angels like, what you did in the Old Testament times and do you really interact with people today? Is it okay if I ask you a few questions? I hope I'm not keeping you from going home." "You know, Anne," he said, "I just don't have that tight of a schedule, you know what I mean?" "Okay, here are the questions, What do angels do; what are your jobs; do you visit humans; who have you visited before; do different angels have different personalities; do you sin, too; do you seek forgiveness, too; what about angel worship?" Then, Robert replied, "Well, first of all, God still keeps lots of secrets from people regarding angels. These secret things are not revealed to people on earth because of their limited capacity to understand. Angels are called Hosts and Jesus repeatedly called Himself the 'Lord of Heavenly Hosts and Lord of Heavenly armies'.

Our main job is to worship God, in fact, all of the souls' main job here in Heaven is to worship God and the humans' main job on earth is to worship God. Angels fear God because we know Him, if you don't fear Him, you don't know Him. Earthly things are going to rust and turn to dust, worshiping God never will. Angels are messengers, comforters, warriors, protectors, servants, deliverers, defenders and ministering spirits. All Heavenly Hosts rejoice for each lost sheep that comes into His fold. Angels assisted men to control kingdoms and appeared as fire or wind. We assisted God's men such as Shadrach, Meschach and Abednego. We helped God's men defeat armies, but sometimes we aren't allowed to interfere when God's people are suffering and are being tormented. God in His infinite wisdom allows it for a greater purpose. They will be rewarded greatly for their suffering, for God will neither leave them nor forsake them. Angels are also messengers. Want to hear a funny story?" "Sure," I said. Robert begins, "Well, about two thousand years ago just before Jesus was born, Mary's relative, Elizabeth, who was old and childless, had always wanted to have a child and God had plans for her."

'Til Tomorrow
Anne Langeman Klassen

67 Hand Signs (Part 2 of 6)

*R*obert continues saying, "In Luke 1:5 it says 'In the time of Herod king of Judea, there was a priest named Zechariah.' Sadly his wife Elizabeth, who both loved God and kept His commandments, didn't have any children and this really bothered her. In those days, being childless was looked on as having divine disfavor and that she had missed out on the joy of raising children to carry on their blood line, but God had plans.

It was Zechariah's turn to keep the incense burning on the altar. The assembled worshipers were praying outside, when Zechariah went inside to the altar in front of the Most Holy Place. Suddenly the angel Gabriel appeared and Zechariah was frightened, which was the usual reaction. Gabriel said, 'Don't be afraid Zechariah, your prayers have been answered. Your wife is going to have a son, you will call him, John. He will be a delight to you and many people will rejoice. He will bring many people of Israel back to the Lord your God and he will go before the Messiah to make people ready for Him.' Listen to this, can you believe it? Zechariah questions the angel's statement and said that he needed a sign because my wife and I are old. Gabriel must have thought; I was sent from God, if you doubt me, then you doubt God. 'Well, how's this for a sign. You won't talk or hear until your son is born. How's that! Now, do you believe?' Here's a senior citizen, who all his life wanted a son and now an angel tells him that his wife will have a very important son, John the Baptist, the messenger who comes before the Messiah and he can't tell anybody about it. Now that's funny! See, angels do have a sense of humor. The message here is: just don't doubt God.

Then I'll bet what happened was that night as old Zechariah was headed home in his chariot to his elderly wife he was thinking, man, I don't know how that angel promise is going to happen. I'm an old man, I'm a senior citizen; when you get this old everything hurts and what doesn't hurt, doesn't work. How am I going to explain to the wife what happened? Let's see. How's this? Honey, I have to use hand signs for everything, but I can explain. See, an angel scared me when I was making sure the incense was burning on the altar and he said something was going to happen and I doubted him and God, so I told him to prove it would come true and to give me a sign. So he made me a sign all right, he made me go deaf and dumb, that's why I'm giving you hand signs instead of talking. And, oh ya, by the way, you're going to get pregnant...Oh, to be a fly on the wall that night at the Zechariah' house and watch Elizabeth's face.

After Elizabeth became pregnant she went into seclusion and celebrated her joy in praise and thanksgiving because in her old age she was going to bear a very important son. Her son, John the Baptist, would be the person chosen by God to preach the coming of the Savior of the world, a miracle birth. Then, the angel Gabriel appeared to Mary, Elizabeth's relative, after Elizabeth had been pregnant about five months. The angel Gabriel announced to Mary that she would bear a son named Jesus.

Isaiah 54:1 "Sing, O barren woman, you who never bore a child; burst into song, shout for joy, you who were never in labor."

Isn't that something
Anne Langeman Klassen

68 Bible Characters (Part 3 of 6)

I asked, "Robert, are angels the same as people?" "No," he said, "People only have limited understanding but some future things are revealed to us angels, such as when we told Mary that she soon would become pregnant and when we told Zechariah that Elizabeth would have a son."

I then asked, "Robert, what was your greatest memory?" "The Ascension Day," he said, " you can't imagine what it was like here knowing Jesus was coming home after being tormented on earth."

"What is your most fun job?" I asked. "The best job," he said, "is going and bringing back the saints-especially if they've suffered for the faith. I just love picking up missionaries, Sunday school teachers, and faithful prayer warriors and then to see them discover when they get here, what an influence they were."

"What was your worst moment ever?" I asked. Robert said that the worst moment was when we were watching the Savior and God turned His back on Jesus when He was on the cross, because Jesus took on the sins of the world. Sin separated the two and Jesus cried out in torment, "Why have You forsaken me?"

"What do you think about humans?" was my next question. Robert said, "I wonder why people are so stubborn and why you don't learn from others' mistakes? You cause yourself so much grief and pain yet you continue doing things that harm you even though the Bible continually warns you what to do and what not to do to have less pain in your life."

"What's your favorite thing to do?" I asked. Then Robert said, "My job is to praise God and do what I'm instructed to do; whether to be a messenger or to be a protector of people or to be a warrior."

141

I asked, "Robert, who were some of the people that the angels have visited that are recorded in the Bible?" "There are many recorded visits," he replied, "The angel Gabriel talked to Mary, the mother of Jesus. We visited Mary's husband, Joseph, in visions three times. We visited shepherds in the field; we visited Daniel in the lion's den; we protected Shadrach, Meshach and Abednego from being burned in the fire. We spoke to Philip; angels talked to Cornelius; we tended to Jesus when He was tempted in the desert, in the Garden of Gethsemane, at the tomb and when He ascended to Heaven. Two angels even stayed behind after Jesus rose up into the clouds. Angels brought Elisha home; predicted Nebachadnezzar's future and we talked to Elijah. It only took one angel to kill one hundred and eighty-five thousand Assyrian soldiers; we talked to Manoah's wife, the mother of Samson; we appeared before Gideon; even Balaam's talking donkey recognized us. We visited Moses and brought his people into God's Promised Land. We visited John and he reports there are over ten thousand times ten thousand angels, at the New Jerusalem. Angels rescued Peter when he was a prisoner and we fed Elijah. We comforted Jesus' mother, Mary, after the crucifixion. We carried the beggar, Lazarus, up to Abraham in Heaven. The guards at the tomb were stunned after they saw us, Jacob and Lot recognized angels. Three of us visited Abraham, an angel wrestled with Jacob and ministered to those who are heirs of salvation. We talked to Philip and told Belshazzar that he had been found wanting and we even helped the servant of Abraham find a bride for Isaac. Angels visited Jacob in a dream in which he saw angels going up and down a ladder to Heaven and angels led the people out of Egypt after forty years in the wilderness.

We appear in visions and dreams quite a bit, but then sometimes we look like humans and you can't tell that we are angels and then sometimes we appear as warriors or messengers. Be careful sometimes Satan can disguise himself as an angel of light because he is a fraud, a liar and a deceiver. The Bible talks about us some three hundred times and we can be visible or invisible Heavenly bodies or spirited bodies. 1 Corinthians 12 talks about angels having their own language and in Jude it says that we have our own place. We can eat food on earth because Sarah gave us roast veal and bread and are sometimes referred to as wind and a flame of fire. We don't have all knowledge but we are told what to do and when to do it. Our garments have been said to be soft, white yet warm of color. Angels can only be in one place at a time but Jesus by His Holy Spirit is omnipresent and He can be in many places at one time, that is how He can visit everyone every day. When He went back to Heaven, He gave you His Holy Spirit."

I then said to Robert, "Let's talk about angels singing," Then he chuckled, "That's kind of a controversial subject to some earthly scholars, isn't it? Let's keep the people guessing? Well, angels don't sing the same as souls sing because we've never experienced saving grace; you see, we were not born into sin. We don't sing of our transgressions being pardoned because we haven't sinned. We can only listen to humans sing about saving grace. We sing praise music and people sing both redemption music and praise music. The Bible doesn't actually say that we sing, it says that we 'say' praises, on the other hand it doesn't say that we don't sing either. You've heard us sing, does that sound like singing, you be the judge. Let's keep your son guessing. I heard David and Brenda played a duet at Langeman Lake the other day that was just beautiful. I hope you recorded that. Brenda asked me to take her to the beach and she mentioned something about water skiing."

The next question is, "Do you know the names of all the angels?" Robert explains, "Well, Michael and Gabriel are the only angels with names in the Bible, except for Lucifer. Michael is the Archangel, he's kind of the enforcer and Gabriel is more involved with delivering news. Angels are called the sons of God. We saw the creation of earth and rejoiced and we don't die; we are timeless.

There are also cherubim, who are ambassadors of God, cherubim also act as guards like when they guarded the Tree of Life in the Garden of Eden and statues of cherubim were placed on the cover of the ark. Seraphim are another form of life in Heaven and their job is to worship God constantly. Angels who are spirit beings are mentioned in the Bible hundreds of times but cherubim and seraphim are mentioned only a few times. God even uses nature itself to praise him, if we won't praise Him, He can even use the rocks to cry out and praise Him.

We worship the God of Creation and we obey Him and do God's work and we are also called Holy Ones in Deuteronomy 33:2. We are protectors of people Psalm 91:11. For He will order His angels to protect you wherever you go. We will never die but God did throw Satan and many of the angels out of Heaven because they wanted to be like God with all the power. Angels also stand protecting Heaven from the fallen angels coming back in. Jesus repeatedly called Himself the Lord of Heavenly armies or the Lord of Hosts which means angels. In 2 Thessalonians 1:7 The Bible says, "the Lord Jesus is revealed from Heaven in blazing fire with His powerful angels."

Fascinating
Anne Langeman Klassen

69 Talking Donkey (Part 4 of 6)

*R*obert told me this story of Balaam from Numbers 22:21-35. Check it out; this really happened. God is angry at Balaam for sinning and the angel of the Lord is sent to kill him as he rides his old faithful donkey down the road. The angel has his sword drawn and Balaam can't see him, but his donkey can. The donkey doesn't want to walk down the path because he sees this fearsome angel who looks like trouble and the donkey was probably thinking, "Hey, wake up boss, you got trouble ahead", so she runs into the field. Then Balaam beats his donkey to get her back on the path. The angel of the Lord then went and stood in the narrow path between two vineyards with walls on both sides. When the poor donkey saw the angel of the Lord again, she thinks to herself here comes trouble again; this isn't good and presses close to the wall, crushing Balaam's foot against the wall. So what does Balaam do, he beats her again. Then the angel of the Lord moves to an area where the donkey can't go left or right, now the donkey just lays down under Balaam. Balaam then takes a rod and beats the poor animal AGAIN.

Then the Lord allows the donkey to talk. Here I paraphrase, "Hello…I'm trying to save your life, what are you doing man, what have I done to deserve that." The funny thing is Balaam actually answers his donkey and said, "If I had a sword in my hand, I would strike you right now." So she replied, "Hey, boss, I've never disobeyed you before. I didn't deserve a beating. Look what I'm seeing!" Then the Lord opened Balaam's eyes and he saw the scary looking angel with his sword drawn. "The donkey was right," the angel said, "she saved your life. I'm going to let you live now, but from now on say only what God wants you to say…got it?"

The donkey probably wasn't too happy with the angel either because she took three beatings; why wasn't one enough? The donkey probably thought, gosh, why couldn't you have let me talk after just one beat down. Man, I've got lumps on my head. At least, somebody should help me register a complaint with the local APDMJ, the Association for the Protection of Donkeys, Mules and Jackasses.

Gerry, if God could use a talking donkey...well!

Ouch
Anne Langeman Klassen

70 Robert's Interview (Part 5 of 6)

I lost six straight games. I rack 'em, I break, he runs the table over and over again, but that's okay because he's giving me a fabulous interview. I said, "Robert, when people first see angels, they are frightened. People find you quite intimidating, especially the warrior angels." Robert answered, "I guess to humans, we can be a bit scary. Mary was frightened by Gabriel, the angel who told her that she would be the mother of the Savior. Almost every time the angels appear before people, their first words seem to be 'Fear not' like in Luke 2:8-20 and when we appeared before the shepherds to tell them that in Bethlehem a Savior had been born, the angels said, 'Do not be afraid.' Then there is the story of the angel's announcement at the tomb that Jesus has risen from the dead, again the angels said, 'Do not be afraid.'

About our appearance- In Matthew 28:3 it says the angels who rolled back the stone from Jesus' tomb had an appearance 'like lightning and his clothes were white as snow' or Mark 16:5 as various men dressed in white robes and two angels in white, John 20:12. 'and two men in clothes that gleamed in lightning, in Luke 24:4. In Acts 1:10 Forty days later there were angels on the ground when Jesus ascended into Heaven and we have appeared to the disciples as two men dressed in white. Colossians 1:16 and Romans 8:37 says that angels have different ranks. Paul speaks of orders of angels and ranks. In Hebrews 13:2 some humans have entertained angels on earth and have not known it. Think about that. You may have already been in contact with an angel on earth and didn't realize it. Makes you think, doesn't it? In Psalm 8:5 David says that man is a little lower than the heavenly beings. In Daniel 9:23 the angel Gabriel visited Daniel and told him the angel's job is to prophesy not preach.

In Matthew 25:31 Jesus says that He will return to earth with his holy angels and in Matthew 13:41-42 it says that Satan will be thrown into the lake of fire where there will be wailing and gnashing of teeth. Jesus said quite a bit about hell and I know it's real; I'm glad you're here and not there. People must rely on mercy from Christ, not justice.

Angels have a more abrupt personality. Kind of like a drill sergeant giving orders in boot camp, we give command statements like; hurry up, rise up, get up, arise and go and go quickly. After God gives the word, we seem to be spirits of action, because angels are organized by God. Anne, like you've found out, we may be a bit mysterious to people, but the mystery is disclosed here in Heaven, isn't it? Luke 2:10-11.

You can read about Paul in 2 Corinthians 12:2-4. He was caught up to Paradise to do a walk about, like the Aussies say, but he was told not to tell what he saw. There were 12 legions of angels surrounding the cross, but we were told not to interfere. Two angels visited Lot and helped him get away from Sodom and Gomorrah just before it was destroyed. Just before dawn angels told Lot to flee with his wife and two daughters or he was going to be swept away when the two cities of Sodom and Gomorrah were punished. Then, in Stephen's last hour he had a face of an angel when he told the council that even though angels have given them the law, they have not kept it, then they stoned him to death and he was given a Heavenly entrance there to receive his crown because he died a martyr. Acts 6:8 and Acts 7:60

Angels only do certain things, we don't preach the same as people preach, maybe it's because we've never felt the agony of being separated from God or the feeling of helplessness of being lost or felt the joy of forgiveness. Angles can't do the same things as humans; maybe that's because we don't have the same emotions as humans. We just have never felt the joy that salvation brings to people but we do bring the message of salvation.

Angels do help preachers, we keep them safe and angels are God's messengers and God's avengers and warriors. Angels never have worry, depression or despair. We number ten thousand times ten thousand. Revelation 5:9-14 and angels rejoice over one sinner who repents. Luke 15:10 Angels serve God just like you did on earth and now here in Paradise. Revelation 19:10 Angels separate the saved from the unsaved. Matthew 13:50 says they shall cast them into the furnace of fire. Angels execute God's judgment and we escort each believer to heaven and welcome each believer like in Luke 16 when we escorted the beggar to Heaven. We share citizenship with the souls in Heaven. Matthew 24:31, and we do have different personalities. We are worship leaders. 1 Corinthians 11:10 We first brought God's message to ordinary people like the shepherds instead of kings in Luke 1:52-53. "many exalted he sent the rich away empty but has given the hungry the good things."

Then I said, "Well, Robert, thank you so very much for sharing your time with me tonight and teaching me pool. Thank you for answering all these questions. Now I am going to find all the people that you talked to and try to get an interview from each one of them, as well. You're such a sweetheart. I just got a book full of information to send to my son." "Oh, Anne, it's been so much fun talking to you. Let's do it again." All of a sudden one of the angels announces, "Hey, guys, I've got the game on at my place!" There was a mighty whoosh and everyone disappeared. Barsuvius was the only angel left in the pool hall, so I asked him, "What just happened?" "We can do that because we are spirits," he said, "Why don't we get two lattes and I'll walk you home?" "Sure, thanks," I said, "Let me straighten up the tab for the table rental. The Times gave me an expense account and I plan on giving it a good workout. Barsuvius, you want a dozen Jamaican patties to go?"

Angels We Have Heard on High
Anne Langeman Klassen

71 Wednesdays (Part 6 of 6)

*A*t the pool hall, we had talked and talked while Robert kept on running the table on me. It got pretty funny after a while, I'd break, he'd run the table, I'd break, he'd run the table. But man, did I get an interview. My recorder ran all afternoon and I've got weeks of work to organize all the information that I've recorded. Before I died I thought that we just rested and did nothing in Heaven. Well, maybe some new arrivals need a little time to settle in, but now I've got two jobs, the decoupage training and the newspaper reporter job. I've never been busier and I just love life.

We were walking back to my place and I wanted to pull some more personal information out of Barsuvius, my angel. I asked him what he enjoyed the most about being an angel. He looked at me and his face just glowed. "I love it when the angel of death calls me and tells me to saddle up my white stallion for I'm to go and bring back a soul. There is nothing that I do that is more fun than that. It's taking people, who have finished running the race, back from death to life. Because of how we look, at first the people are a little startled by our appearance, but when I tell them who sent me, the reaction is mixed, from trepidation, caution, wonder, joy, excitement, but mostly it is YES, I'm headed home. I get them to climb up on the back of my horse and away we go."

Then I asked what is it that you don't like about your job? His shoulders slumped and he looked uncomfortable. I had to be careful here, because it looked like I had ventured into very tender territory. "Wednesdays," he said, "Wednesdays, I don't like Wednesdays." "Don't ask," I said to myself, "let him volunteer it." As far as I know they don't cry, but this is as close to sorrow and anguish as

I've seen from an angel. "Wednesdays is when I have to go to the clinic... That's when I pick up God's tiny souls whose discarded lives were sacrificed...whose death was scheduled."

Jesus loves the little children,
All the children of the world,
Red and yellow, black and white
All are precious in His sight.
Jesus loves the little children of the world.

Mercy
Anne Langeman Klassen

72 Camping Trip

*G*erry, this is the last letter for a little while, because Dan and I are taking the Harley out to the desert and we're only taking a pup tent. We're going to go out and just lie on a blanket and watch cumulus clouds form and watch hawks soar in thermals. Have you ever watched a cloud form? Do it for me today. Just stare at one cloud and watch God make it and then dissipate it. Maybe you and I will be looking at the same cloud.

I hope you've enjoyed reading these letters from Heaven half as much as I've enjoyed writing them for you. As you have seen, the main theme in my letters is Jesus' love which is life everlasting. Everybody dies, I fought it as long as I could, you will fight it, and everybody else will battle against the angel of death. I was welcomed into Paradise and there was not one thing that I did to earn my way in. Only the saving grace of Jesus, the redeeming blood of the Lamb, allowed me to live where I'm living today, in Jesus' house. He allows everybody to either accept or reject Him, and we never know the hour that rejection becomes final. It's like when God closed up the ark, sealed the door and the rains started falling. It was too late for the inhabitants outside of the ark. The ship floated away and nothing that his neighbors cried out would allow that door to be reopened, because God had sealed it shut. I beg you to get your admission ticket to walk up the boarding plank before the door is shut. Nothing you will ever do will be more life changing.

Brenda heard about our plans for the weekend and begged Dan to let her come with us. Right away Dan agreed. He just loves the little souls. Then Brenda asked Molly if she wanted to go with us too. Brenda said they could both fit in the motorcycle side car, so Dan said okay.

Then Molly asked Frieda to go with us, Frieda asked your Oma and Opa, Oma asked your Aunt Mary, so I called Clayton, Clayton called Spyder Koop, Spyder called Barsuvius, my angel, but he's busy taking care of a single mother in Somalia. Brenda contacted little Timmy and he's coming. Timmy, Brenda and Molly all live with Jesus in the mansion with many rooms. Oma asked Mary and my sister Mary asked Moses if he wanted to go because he likes the solitude of the desert and he said, "Sure." I guess we'll just rent some RV's to accommodate everybody. Opa asked Pete if he wanted to go and he's bringing a trailer full of off road vehicles. He's also bringing some of his trail horses from his ranch because Brenda begged him. She loves riding horses. We are also going to stop at Gabriel's paragliding school. His place is located where you come over the mountain and look down toward the desert floor-it's right there. The wind hits the side of the mountain just right, so you get lift and later on in the day when the thermals pick up, you can circle in the lift all the way up to the cloud base. We're all going to stop and give it a try. I'm so excited about this. There is a large area for camping at *Gabriel's Paragliding Park*, so we may stay there the first night.

I've got to go to the grocery store this afternoon and pick up some food supplies. When you're camping out, there's nothing like bacon and eggs and a pot of coffee over an open fire in the morning. I'm really looking forward to this weekend. I'm glad Moses is coming because that gives me all weekend to interview him. I've been getting interviews from Mary, the Mother of Jesus, about what it was like when she was raising Jesus. I see her at my decoupage classes so I'll be sending you those interviews when I get back from the desert next week. Here's the characters I'll be interviewing in the next few weeks. There's Luke, Isaac, Elizabeth, Mary Magdalene, Samson,

Solomon, King David, Paul, John the Baptist, Daniel and the famous Adam and Eve. I'll write soon.

Redeemed by the Blood of the Lamb
Anne Langeman Klassen

—◈—

For a Christian everything turns out great in the end. If it hasn't turned out great… it is not the end.

"Surely goodness and love will follow me
all the days of my life, and I will dwell in the
house of the LORD forever."
Psalm 23:6

A FUNNY THING HAPPENED TO THE AUTHOR

~~~

I'm sitting in my writing chair as dawn is approaching and there's just a little bit of red under the horizon. A thought came over me that I wanted to share with you. We just sent the draft of this book to the publisher and I'm taking a look back at what was my privilege in writing this parable book of letters from my mom. First of all, from the bottom of my heart, thank you for taking your time to read what was absolutely the most fun experience in my entire life. I'm looking back and not one single time did I get frustrated or impatient or angry, which this sad soul is apt to do. Not one time was there anything but pure joy. I was wondering what was making the difference between this and my real job, the one that's supposed to put bread on the table. Well, I came to the conclusion that it's my quiet time with Him. For once, I quit talking and started listening. He was telling me the answers; before I had just been too loud to hear the answers.

You know the type of motorcycle driven by Dad in Heaven, doesn't matter. Whether Mom plays fast ball or hard ball, or whether the angels play billiards or eight ball

159

really is of no consequence. What this book is really all about is my Savior's love for you and me and His free gift of salvation for the sin sick soul and if that came across, I'm a happy man.

I want to publicly thank my sister, Verna and my wife, Anne. Without you two forcefully prodding, this book would still be, "Ya, you know, you should write a book someday." I love you both with all that I am. My greatest desire is not to see how many books are sold, but how many times souls are affected. It may make an eternal difference in one life, when you share these thoughts with others.

If I never meet you or hear from you on earth... because I've got a whole lot more days behind me than in front of me, let's make a date to meet at Langeman's Lake at Peter's concession stand. I'll be there first thing in the morning picking up some bait and renting a row boat. See, I'm planning on going fishing with my grandkids and Brenda and Molly for the first hundred thousand years, and I'll see if I can pick up a part-time job helping my mom with her news reporter work, maybe she can make me a junior reporter.

In Christ Alone, I Take My Stand
Gerry-Son of Anne Klassen

CAST OF CHARACTERS

Anne Klassen : lives in Heaven; co-author; decoupage instructor; reporter for Beulah Land Times

Dan Klassen: faithful husband of Anne; sings in The Thirst Quencher Quartet

Oma: Anne's mother; takes care of her Heavenly garden

Opa: Anne's father; lives with Oma and rides his Harley Davidson

Verna, Margaret, and Janet: Anne's daughters here on earth; Anne's pride and joy

Gerry: wife's name is also Anne, who is the greatest wife in the whole wide world; author

Kirra and Delaney: Anne's great-granddaughters from Gerry' son, Darren and his wife, Kelley

Van: Anne's great-grandson from Gerry's son, Bryce and his wife, Miranda

Clayton: son of Janet; lives in Heaven; operates *the Safe and Sound Skateboarding School*; gives his grandmother Anne rides on his Harley

Mary: Anne's sister; who is an artist in Heaven

Pete: Anne's brother; owns ranch that overlooks Langeman Lake in Heaven

Frieda: Anne's sister; enjoys waterskiing in Heaven; wife of Rudy; mother of Leonard who was Gerry's best friend in their youth

Rudy: Frieda's husband; sings in the Thirst Quencher Quartet in Heaven with Dan

Lilia: Anne's friend on earth

Angelika: Anne's friend on earth

Bible characters

Noah: ark builder; cruise ship director in Heaven

Adam and Eve: everybody's original parents

Peter: disciple of Jesus; runs Langeman Lake concession stand; ski instructor

Mark: disciple of Jesus; partner of Peter at Langeman Lake concession stand; ski instructor

Pontius Pilate: Jesus' judge before the crucifixion

Judas: disciple of Jesus; betrayed Jesus before crucifixion

Gabriel: messenger angel; worships God

Michael: warrior angel; worships God; the Archangel

David: King on earth; author; great story teller; musician; teaches boys about how to use sling shots

Lady at the Well: met Jesus at the well and received soul quenching water

Lazarus: rose from the dead; died twice

Job: suffered on earth; has psychiatrist office in Heaven but no clients

Ezekiel: plays third base on Ageless Ambassadors baseball team

Methuselah: a senior citizen; center fielder on Ageless Ambassadors baseball team

Fictional Characters

Angel Barsuvius: Anne's angel; retrieves souls on his white horse

Molly: little soul; imp; laughs a lot

Brenda: little soul; leader of the imps; mischievious

Tommy: little soul; loves to ride the train

Yytsag: Dan's New York friend

Bostock: one of the lead angels; very strong

Angelo: Roman soldier who helped crucify Christ

Marcus: a shepherd; saw the miracle Messiah

Tarek: little soul on the motorcycle trip

George: a shepherd who failed the Mensa exam

Frankie: Runs the Five Loaves and Two Fishes concession at the Eastern Gate

Britney: little soul at the library; trickster

Grandpa Grabowski: Harley rider with side car; loves little souls

Timmy: rides in side car with Grandpa Grabowski

Fauntleroy aka Bubba: first base on Ageless Ambassadors baseball team

Willard: angel who went on motorcycle trip; retrieved Martha from Russia that night

Buster: little soul on motorcycle trip

Robert: angel at Paradise Pool and Cue; pool shark; gave Anne a long interview

Spyder Koop: friend of Anne and Dan; lives near them in Heaven; bass singer

George Strathroy: retired GM engineer

Robert DeMarco: owner of classic 1957 Chevy